The Persian Invasions of Greece

The Persian Invasions of Greece

Arthur Keaveney

Pen & Sword
MILITARY

First published in Great Britain in 2011 by
Pen & Sword Military
an imprint of
Pen & Sword Books Ltd
47 Church Street
Barnsley
South Yorkshire
S70 2AS

Copyright © Arthur Keaveney 2011

ISBN 978-1-84884-137-6

The right of Arthur Keaveney to be identified as Author of this Work
has been asserted by him in accordance with the Copyright, Designs
and Patents Act 1988.

A CIP catalogue record for this book is available from the British
Library.

Typeset in 11pt Ehrhardt by
Mac Style, Beverley, E. Yorkshire

Printed and bound in the UK by CPI

Pen & Sword Books Ltd incorporates the Imprints of Pen & Sword
Aviation, Pen & Sword Family History, Pen & Sword Maritime, Pen &
Sword Military, Pen & Sword Discovery, Wharncliffe Local History,
Wharncliffe True Crime, Wharncliffe Transport, Pen & Sword Select,
Pen & Sword Military Classics, Leo Cooper, The Praetorian Press,
Remember When, Seaforth Publishing and Frontline Publishing

For a complete list of Pen & Sword titles please contact
PEN & SWORD BOOKS LIMITED
47 Church Street, Barnsley, South Yorkshire, S70 2AS, England
E-mail: enquiries@pen-and-sword.co.uk
Website: www.pen-and-sword.co.uk

Contents

Acknowledgements

There are three people I wish to thank for help in making this book. Philip Sidnell commissioned the work and showed patience with a moderately tardy author. Although she has no palaeographical training, Kirsty Corrigan deciphered my handwriting and produced the typescript. My wife Jenny took many of the photos and also shared the burden of proof-reading. Rath Dé orthu go léir.

List of Plates

List of Maps

Map 1: The Aegean, circa 500 BC.

Prologue: Greeks and Persians

This book tells of the attempt by the great Achaemenid Empire of Ancient Persia to conquer the states of Greece and of its failure.

To this day Greece and Persia (Iran) exist, old civilisations, justly proud of their ancestors and their history. But that history has been a long one and much has changed in the interval of over two thousand years. We must, therefore, begin by describing how affairs stood then for both peoples.

By the time at which our narrative begins – roughly the mid-sixth century BC – Greece had already witnessed the flourishing and fall of two great civilisations, the Minoan and Mycenaen. These great palace cultures flourished successively between 2000 and 1200 BC but had vanished by the second half of the twelfth century BC when the Mycenaens collapsed in the face of invaders from the north. There then followed a period of great obscurity for us which we, in consequence, dub the dark ages of Greece. About 850 BC these come to an end.

It is at this point that we first catch a glimpse of the lineaments of Greek statehood and culture. What we are witnessing is a conglomerate of states of varying size. Although sharing a common language and revering a common pantheon, these states never achieved political unity. That was not to come until it was imposed by the Macedonians in the fourth century BC. What did come about was emigration. Scarcity of land and the opportunity of trade ensured that the Greeks now spread over the Mediterranean and founded colonies. This was the second time such had occurred. About 1000 BC there had been a migration, lasting some hundred or so years, to Ionia in Asia Minor. The states founded there will figure prominently in our story but first there is more to say about Greek history and habits.

Generalisations inevitably bring exceptions with them but the following broad sketch may be offered. At the end of the dark ages we find the states of Greece governed by kings but soon they mostly fade away. Their place is taken by aristocracy. These are oligarchs who claim to rule by right of birth. Their wealth comes from their great estates and they dominate warfare. In these times cavalry was the chief weapon and only the rich nobility could afford to keep and maintain horses. In turn, however, the aristocracy were displaced by new men who had grown rich by trade and adopted a new style of warfare: infantry. The heavily armoured Greek soldier now came into his own. This new movement also threw up the tyrant. At this time this word did not carry with it the sinister connotations of the present day. Rather it referred to a man who ruled illegally but often benignly. The age of tyrants in the Greek homeland did not endure beyond a couple of generations but lasted longer in the cities of Asia Minor, a circumstance which again will concern us.

With the end of the age of tyranny we find most of the Greek states, on the eve of the Persian invasions, possessing political systems where power was now more evenly distributed among their inhabitants. To a greater or lesser degree, the people in their assemblies governed. These assemblies formed an integral part of the structure of the city state. To the Greeks the city was the optimal form of existence. Aristotle's dictum that man is a political animal is well known but must be interpreted in the broadest sense. As the citizen of a *polis* or city a man would take part not only in its political life but also in its cultural and religious activities. By playing his part to the full he would achieve the rounded ideal.

Such, in outline, was the Greek world.[1] We turn now to the Persians and give them a slightly fuller treatment. No apology is necessary for this. The Greeks have long been a subject of study and hence knowledge of them is long widely diffused. It is otherwise with Achaemenid Persia. Scholarly interest in it has not been as intense or as prolonged. Hence for many people the ancient Iranians are still mysterious or simply misunderstood.

The Persians were ruled by a king who, like most monarchs, governed by divine right. A man was king in Persia and king of the lands – the term empire was not used – by the grace of Ahura Mazda, the god of the Iranians. In his person the king was held to embody to the greatest degree all of the attributes of the Persian male, beauty, physical strength, mastery of the bow and the horse, devotion to the Truth and enmity to the Lie.

The king was an absolute ruler in the lands he ruled over. Unquestioning obedience was required from his subjects who were bound to him by a tie of loyalty called *bandaka*. The Greeks who, as we saw, were masters of their own affairs and prized their freedom, professed to see in this a state of total slavery. But when we learn that Persian rule was light and mild, and compare the lot of those who lived under it with that, say, of the helots in Sparta, then we might very well conclude that life in the Persian empire was sometimes happier than that in a Greek state.

For one man to rule so great an empire would prove difficult, so the king resigned a portion of his authority to others. The empire was parcelled out into provinces called satrapies which were governed by officials called satraps. Although subordinate to the king they enjoyed a considerable measure of power. Two principal checks to this power were the secretary and the garrison commander who were under the direct command of the king. Flow of information to court was achieved by a courier system, the wonder of the world then and now, which operated chiefly on the Royal Road between Sardis and Susa.

So far as the king himself was concerned there existed three checks on his absolutism. He might, and sometimes did, seek advice from members of the court. One instance once encountered tends not to be forgotten. Cambyses wished to marry his sister and asked a panel of experts if it was lawful for him to do so. As Cambyses was of a morose and savage disposition the reply was prudent: no law said a man might marry his sister but the king of Persia was permitted to do as he pleased.[2] And, to anticipate, we shall in the course of this book find other instances of consultation during the invasions.

The second check on the king came from the influence of strong personalities about him. We will find that men like Mardonius enjoyed a certain influence with Xerxes, and some of the later Achaemenids are said to have been hag ridden and in the power of their mothers and wives.

The third check was assassination. As we shall soon see, the king's security service was excellent and protected him from external enemies. The threat, therefore, came from within. The king, especially in the later period of Achaemenid rule, could be at the mercy of ambitions of younger brothers who felt they had a better claim to the throne than he. Such cadets were often aided by or urged on by servants and ministers of the court.

Another strong contrast with the Greeks is found in the fact that the Persians resided in palaces, not cities. In these palace complexes, king and nobility lived surrounded by courtiers, ministers, servants and guards. Chief among the often ceremonial officers were some with self-explanatory titles such as the Cup Bearer and the Bow Carrier. By far the most important of the officials was the *chiliarch* or commander of a thousand men. The king had an elite bodyguard of ten thousand called the Immortals because when one, for whatever reason, dropped out he was immediately replaced. At any one time a thousand were on duty, hence the name of the commander.

The *chiliarch* controlled access to the king. Each visitor had to satisfy him that he had legitimate business with his master. The visitor was then taken to an inner court and into the hands of the ushers. Once in the presence of the king he had to perform *proskynesis*. This was a bow and a kiss performed as a gesture of respect. To the Greeks however it was abhorrent because they mistakenly believed the king was being treated as a god.

The ritual we have just described together with the fact that the king often took his meals hidden behind a curtain have led to the conclusion that he lived in seclusion. But this was not total: for instance, he played a full part in one of the main pastimes of the court: lion hunting, which took place in 'paradises' or game parks that were maintained near the palaces, and were places full of trees, lush vegetation and running water for then, as now, the Persians delighted in gardens. Further, the court was peripatetic, moving with the seasons between Susa, Babylon, Ecbatana and Persepolis. On such circuits the king showed himself to his people and, on occasion, graciously received in audience an individual subject.

Persia was a warrior society. The term 'macho' is easily applied to it when we discover that every year the king gave prizes to those who had excelled in battle or fathered the most children. It was also hierarchical. The king, of course, stood at the apex but those below him were carefully graded. When Persians met they would indicate, by the form of greeting used, how they stood vis-à-vis each other with respect to rank.

The delight in greenery we mentioned above is, to a great extent, to be attributed to the religion of the Persians which enjoined care of the earth upon its followers. There is much debate among experts as to how that religion is to be characterized. At one extreme are those who wish to call it Zoroastrianism pure and simple. At the other extreme are those who wish to label it Mazdaism because, as we saw, the Persians acknowledged Ahura Mazda as their great god. Others again opt for a middle way. They believe that what we have here in the Achaemenid period is either an unorthodox or underdeveloped form of Zoroastrianism.

However we choose to label or categorize it, it is important for us to know something about this religion for, here again, we have one of those things which most strictly mark off Persian and Greek. As we just saw, the ancient Persians believed in a supreme god, Ahura Mazda who was clothed in the sky. He was assisted by six Spentas or creations who were immanent in elements such as water or fire and may be roughly equated with the angels of Christian belief. Unlike the Greeks, the Persians did not conceive of their gods in anthropomorphic shape. Hence they made no statues and erected no temples. Sacrifices were made and prayers said before fire altars but, contrary to vulgar opinion, the Achaemenids did not worship fire but revered it as the most sacred of the elements. In this they are at one with Zoroastrians of the present day, but they differ from them not only in the practice of blood sacrifice but in acknowledging other gods besides Ahura Mazda. Where both agree, however, is in their strongly dualistic nature. Both recognize the existence of an evil force, Ahriman, which is in perpetual conflict with Ahura Mazda.

Man, in this belief, has a choice: he may side with Ahura Mazda or with Ahriman in the struggle. In consequence Persian society is permeated by a strong ethical element. Lying and untruth are abhorred and there is a great preoccupation with justice. The king is the source of all justice and we find him, in judging a man, weighing up the good and bad he has done before deciding his fate. And as with the satrapies, too, he resigned a portion of his competence in this sphere to others. The Persians had a developed system of justice. Judges, appointed by the king, strictly administered the laws.[3]

Such then are the two peoples whose conflict will be narrated in this book. In our next chapter we will tell of their first encounters and discover that, from the outset, they met in no friendly fashion.

Chapter 1

From Cyrus to Darius

The Persians are believed to have travelled from the East about 1000 BC accompanied by their cousins, the Medes. The latter took up residence in what is now in the northwest of present-day Iran and in part of Azerbaijan, while the Persians themselves eventually settled in what is now modern Fars. They are both mentioned in Assyrian records from the ninth and eighth century BC respectively. The Assyrians, a people noted especially for their cruelty, were the great and dominant power of the day. But, as that power began to fade, the Medes and the Babylonians turned on their masters and, with the destruction of their capital Nineveh in 612 BC, the Assyrian dominance came to an end.

The Medes were plainly in a buoyant mood for they now advanced westward against the great power of Asia Minor, Lydia. Six campaigns were fought until a battle which took place in either 585 or 582 was interrupted by an eclipse. This seems to have been enough for both sides and a treaty was made fixing the boundary between the two kingdoms at the Halys River. Some believe the Babylonians, anxious to maintain the balance of power in the region, brokered the peace.

In all of this we hear nothing of the Persians since they appear to have been in some kind of state of subordination to the Medes. That was to change when Cyrus II became ruler of the Persians in 550 BC.[1]

The story of the youth of Cyrus and how he came to overthrow the power of the Medes had, by the time it reached Herodotus, our chief source, already entered the realm of the folktale. The story, as he tells it, goes as follows.

Astyages, the king of the Medes, had a dream which he was told meant evil would come to him from his daughter Mandane. So he married her off to a Persian called Cambyses. Then, when she became pregnant, Astyages had another dream which portended her child would become king one day. He therefore resolved to make away with it, lest it supplant him. Seemingly he could not bring himself to do the actual deed. So he gave the job to his steward Harpagus. He, in turn, baulked at the notion of carrying out this commission and turned the child over to a herdsman to have it exposed on a hillside. The herdsman brought the baby home where he discovered his own wife had given birth to a dead child. So he substituted this child for the one he had been given and showed it to Harpagus to prove the deed had been done.

In this way, Cyrus escaped his would-be murderers and grew to boyhood. One day he was playing at king and courtiers in the street and, when one of his playmates disobeyed him, Cyrus had him chastised. The boy's father complained to Astyages and Cyrus was brought before him. Astyages immediately recognized him as his grandson. He set about interrogating the herdsman and then Harpagus. When the whole story came out, he placed the chief blame on the steward and devised a gruesome revenge. He had Harpagus' son killed and served up to him at a banquet and, in so doing, laid up trouble for himself. He then made enquiries about the possibility of Cyrus' becoming king and was assured that the dream had been amply fulfilled when Cyrus played at king in the street and that there was nothing further to be feared from that quarter, so he sent him back to his parents in Persia. As with Harpagus' dinner, this, too, was to prove a bad mistake.

Among the Persians, Cyrus as a young man became prominent. Harpagus, who had a score to settle with Astyages, eventually entered into a treasonable correspondence with him promising his aid and that of other disaffected Median nobles should he rise up against his master. As the Persians were chafing under Median dominance, Cyrus found it easy to muster the host. As he advanced on the enemy, Astyages stupidly put Harpagus in charge of his army only to find that the majority of the troops who were in the plot ran away. Astyages then put himself at the head of another army only to go down to defeat.

It will be appreciated that there are a good deal of fantastic elements in the above account but one historical fact emerges without doubt: Cyrus had overthrown the power of the Medes and replaced it with that of the Persians. The rest of our tradition enables us to catch a glimpse – at times albeit elusive – of a generally attractive personality. The Persians, undoubtedly, were capable of random and occasional acts of cruelty but never exhibited the systematic savagery of their predecessors, the Assyrians. Cyrus himself was undoubtedly a tough and ruthless warrior but proved himself chivalrous to fallen opponents. Astyages, and later the Lydian king Croesus, were allowed to live and generous provisions were made for the upkeep of their households, which were still on a princely scale. The Persians whom he had brought to power naturally revered him greatly but such reverence also extended to those he ruled over since his rule was seen as mild, tolerant in matters of religion, and beneficent. The Jews especially esteemed him since he released them from captivity in Babylon and gave permission for the Temple to be rebuilt. The prophet known as the second Isaiah even goes so far as to hail him as the 'messiah'. From Babylon, too, there comes a text known as the Cyrus Cylinder, in which he guarantees the rights and wellbeing of the citizens. Some even go so far as to see in this declaration the first charter of human rights.

But, whatever his personality, Cyrus was the founder of the Persian Empire. We often style it the Achaemenid Empire, since this was the house to which he and his successors belonged. After subduing the Medes, Cyrus, in turn, conquered Lydia and Babylon, as well as extending the boundaries of the empire eastwards almost to India. The first of these conquests was Lydia and this came about as a result of a war of aggression by the Lydians themselves against Cyrus.[2]

Before going on to describe this war, something more must be said about Croesus, the king of Lydia, and his dynasty, the Mermnadae, in order to better understand how these events impacted on the Greeks.

The Mermnadae, according to legend, had supplanted the previous dynasty, the Heraclids, in rather interesting circumstances. The last Heraclid king, Candaules, was apparently actually in love with his own wife. Besotted with her beauty, he desired that one of his courtiers, Gyges, should see that beauty for himself and look upon her naked. Gyges sneaked into the royal bedroom and saw but was himself seen by the queen. She threatened to have him killed if he did not kill Candaules. Gyges chose the lesser of two evils and killed his master. He then consulted Delphi, who approved the deed but warned retribution would come to his house in the fifth generation. In time, those who interested themselves in such things realized that Croesus and his fate were in question.

Although he sent presents to Delphi, Gyges nonetheless determined to add the Greek cities of the coast of Asia Minor – those we mentioned in our prologue – to his kingdom and to this end attacked Miletus and Smyrna, but to no avail. His son Ardys took Priene but fared no better than his father at Miletus. Sadyattes, his successor, took Smyrna but he too failed at Miletus. A lengthy siege here was continued by the next king, Alyattes. In the course of the siege he fell ill and was cured after taking the advice of the Delphic Oracle, to whom he sent gifts, before eventually concluding peace with the Milesians.

We can now see a pattern emerging. The Mermnadae had phil-Hellenic tendencies and a respect for Greek culture but this did not stop them from attempting to enlarge their dominions by subduing those Greek cities which were nigh and abiding. In Croesus both of these facets of their rule can be seen with the greatest clarity. He succeeded where his ancestors had failed and brought the Greeks to heel. At the same time he gave the clearest proofs of phil-Hellenism.

He first tried to discover which Greek oracle was the most trustworthy. To this end he sent messengers round to enquire what he was doing on a particular day. Only the Delphic Oracle got it right and, in his delight, Croesus sent most magnificent gifts to the shrine. About the same time he sought out the strongest state in Greece, Sparta, and made an alliance with her.[3]

This last detail showed there was an element of calculation in all this. Croesus had determined to make war on Persia. Not only was he worried by her growing power but he had a personal reason for action. Astyages was his brother-in-law. In order to discover how things would turn out, Croesus sent to Delphi to ask what would happen if he attacked the Persians. He was told he would destroy a great empire. Without pausing to ask which empire that might be, he marched off against the Persians (547 BC). In the event, the empire which would be destroyed would be his own.

Somewhere in Cappadocia the two sides met in a great battle which went on till nightfall. Croesus had the worst of it and began a retreat. His aim was to hole up in Sardis for the winter and summon his allies for a spring campaign but he misjudged the temperament of his opponent. Usually ancient armies did not fight in winter but Cyrus disregarded the norm and followed in pursuit. A second battle followed before Sardis itself, where Croesus was thoroughly beaten and obliged to take refuge in the citadel to await his allies. They never came. Arguably the greatest taker of towns and fortresses before the fourth century BC, the Persians soon stormed the place.[4]

Croesus' fate is of some interest. Hearing he was a god-fearing man, Cyrus put him alive on a funeral pyre in order, it would seem, to discover if his deities would save him. As it turns out they did. Croesus called on the Delphian Apollo who sent a shower of rain which doused the flames. Impressed, Cyrus took him into his service and kept him about the place ever after as a special advisor.[5]

The Greeks of Asia now had a new master and they waited upon Cyrus to ask if they might continue to enjoy, under him, the same status as they had had under Croesus. Unfortunately they had miscalculated, presumably believing so great a power as that of Lydia could not be overturned by these new warriors from out of the East. In the previous year Cyrus had tried to detach them from Croesus with fair terms and only Miletus had agreed. Cyrus now told them the parable of the piper and the fishes. A piper once went down to the sea and played to the fish to make them dance but got no response. Next day, he came back with a net and, as he watched his catch flounder, he told them it was too late to dance now when they would not do so when he had played to them.[6]

Receiving this broad hint of things to come, the Ionians came together at the Panionion at Mycale on the mainland opposite Samos. Delegates had been accustomed to meet here for religious ceremonies and gradually gatherings had assumed a political complexion. The unkind said the whole thing never amounted to more than a talking-shop. Be that as it may, it was now resolved to send to Sparta for help. The Spartans were, it would seem, unwilling to get involved, but felt they had to do something so they made a gesture. They sent one ship with ambassadors to Cyrus and warned him to keep his hands off the Greeks of Asia. Flabbergasted at this insolence, Cyrus asked who these people were and, on being told, said he had no fear of a people who went down to the agora to cheat each other. He would soon give them troubles enough of their own so that they would not need to concern themselves with those of others.[7]

At this point, Cyrus headed off to attend to business in the east. Scarcely was he on the road, when his governor of Lydia, Pactyes, rose in revolt. Recruiting from the cities of the coast, he laid siege to Sardis. Cyrus sent Mazares the Mede against him and he was eventually betrayed by the Chians. Once Mazares had quitted Lydia, he turned his attentions to Ionia. He took and enslaved Priene and then subdued Magnesia and the plain of the Maeander. After his death the command was given to Harpagus, who began a systematic campaign of sieges of the towns which fell to him one by one. Two communities decided they had had enough and fled. The Teans made it to Thrace, where they founded the city of Abdera. Some of the Phoceans repented of the decision to move and returned home. The remainder of them headed for the western Mediterranean, where they were to become a nuisance to their neighbours by indulging in piracy.

While Harpagus was about his work, meetings continued at the Panionion where various options were discussed to no avail. One proposal was to form a federal government centred on Teos. And after the subjugation another emerged which, again in vain, counselled that all the Ionians relocate en masse to Sardinia.

And the surrender of many of the islands soon followed that of the mainland, as the frightened inhabitants yielded. In this way, then, the Greeks of Asia came under the dominance of Persia.[8]

Cyrus himself never returned to Asia Minor but busied himself with those conquests which, in the short space of thirty years, established the Persian empire and made of it a great power. He perished (529 BC) while on campaign in the eastern marches of his dominions and was succeeded by his son Cambyses who reigned between 529–522 BC. His most notable achievement was the conquest of Egypt but, so far as we know, he had no significant dealings with the Greeks.[9]

Cambyses died in an accident on the way home from Egypt. He was hurrying to deal with a usurper called Smerdis who, it was believed, was passing himself off as Cambyses' dead brother. The tale is a complicated one because, nowadays anyway, many think the man really was Cambyses' brother and that the story of imposture was put about by those who, as we shall see in a moment, had strong motives for doing so. Smerdis ruled for seven months, when a group of nobles claimed to have finally discovered that he was a fraud and duly assassinated him. At the head of the conspiracy stood a man called Darius who now became king.

It is sometimes thought this man may have had a hand in spreading the rumour that Smerdis was not who he claimed to be.

Darius was not a descendant of Cyrus but belonged to a cadet branch of the Achaemenids and had to work hard to establish his credentials and lay emphasis on his connections with the ruling house.

Nor, initially, do the peoples of the empire seem to have been impressed by him. Smerdis had been popular – among other things he had remitted taxes – and the opportunity to be free of Persian rule seemed too good to miss. In the first year of his reign (522–521 BC), Darius is recorded as having fought nineteen battles and dealt with nine rebel kings. This was not the end of it, but by 518 BC Darius had seen off every challenge and had established himself firmly on the throne.

Darius, though, is not just remembered as a warrior. In the history of the Persian empire he is, arguably, second in importance only to Cyrus. A great administrator, he stamped his image on the empire and gave it the form it was to have until its overthrow by Alexander the Great some two centuries later.

Under his predecessors, satrapies or provinces had existed, but Darius now increased their number to twenty. At the head of each stood a governor or satrap. Given that these men had the potential to rebel, Darius kept control of their secretaries and garrison commanders. He also established the tribute for every part of the empire and decreed it should be fixed and immutable. No provision was made for changing economic circumstances. This same interest in matters economic led Darius to institute the first Persian money, a gold coin called the Daric. The building of a canal to the Red Sea and exploratory expeditions to the western Mediterranean, North Africa and the Indian Ocean have been interpreted as attempts to stimulate trade. Be that as it may, the Persians themselves made no secret of what they thought of Darius' activities in the economic sphere. Cyrus they said was a father, Cambyses a tyrant, but Darius was a shopkeeper. Cyrus was honoured as the founder of the empire, Cambyses execrated for his erratic temper but Darius was castigated for an unhealthy interest in commerce. The habitual hauteur of the great Persian noble could ill-brook meddling in what was properly the concern of the lowly and the grubby.[10]

These slanders were unjustified. The man who had seen off so many rebels at the beginning of his reign certainly did not propose to spend the rest of it in peaceful pursuits, however beneficial they might be to his subjects. The early Achaemenids appear to have had some kind of ideology of conquest. The king was expected to make aggressive war in order to prove himself and Darius did not intend to be an exception. Where Cyrus and Cambyses had led, he proposed to follow in turn.

He found what he was looking for in the Scyths of what is today south Russia. Long before, they had attacked the Medes, and Darius now proposed to take revenge for this, although his brother, Artabanus, whose cautious disposition we shall meet with again in the time of Xerxes, advised against it. Ignoring his brother, Darius gathered a land and sea force. As he marched to the Bosphorus, a Persian noble asked that one of his sons might be allowed to stay at home. Darius said they all might and then had them put to death. Reaching the Bosphorus at Chalcedon, he crossed over by a bridge which had been built by an Ionian, Mandrocles, whom Darius loaded with presents for his work.

The king then marched into Thrace and conquered a part of it. The Getae, a warlike tribe, resisted but were crushed. In this way, Darius came to the Danube after having left in his wake a series of pillars extolling his deeds. The fleet, composed of Greeks drawn from the coast of Asia Minor, had been sent ahead. At the rendezvous, another bridge was made ready for the crossing. Darius is said to have contemplated destroying it in his wake. This seems somewhat unlikely but the account goes on to say that, in any case, he was dissuaded by Coes of Mytilene, who pointed out the obvious dangers.

Crossing over, Darius left the Ionians to guard the bridge, telling them to destroy it if he had not returned in sixty days. At first sight, this may have seemed a risky decision, but not if we look at it from the Persian viewpoint. They were subjects who were expected to obey and there was no reason to suppose they would behave in any way differently from the other subject peoples.

Darius' campaign was not a success. We need not go into great detail since much of what happened is not immediately relevant to our theme. The Scythians poisoned the wells and destroyed pasturage. They then withdrew before the Persians and, refusing to stand and fight, led them a deadly dance across the steppes. Next they worked their way around behind the enemy and, coming to the bridge, urged the Ionians to break it down within the agreed period of sixty days. To this the Ionians agreed. Eventually, when Darius, with his severely damaged army, decided to retreat, the Scythians came again to the bridge and, declaring the sixty days up, urged the Ionians to act.

There then followed a debate typical of such a disputatious people. In order to fully appreciate this, it must be recalled that the Greek contingents were led by tyrants, men who, with the support of Persia, were sole rulers in their own states. One of these was a man called Miltiades. Due to the enmity of the Pisistratids who ruled Athens as tyrants at this time, he had gone to the Chersonese and there established a tyranny of his own. He now proposed they follow the Scythians' advice. He seemed about to prevail when another tyrant, Histiaeus of Miletus, intervened and drew attention to one fundamental fact: they ruled by the grace and favour of the Persians. Should they go down, then the tyrants would go down with them.

This brought people to their senses. In order to fool the Scythians, the Greeks removed part of the bridge, pretending they were about the business of demolition. They then prevailed upon the Scythians to go back in search of the Persians. They failed, however, to make contact and Darius was able to struggle back to the bridge to be ferried across to safety.[11]

He now made his way homeward via Thrace. He left there a large force under one of his generals, Megabazus. This man began his campaign by reducing Perinthus on the Hellespont and then moved on to conquer a large part of Thrace. This brought him to the borders of Macedonia whose subjection is the subject of a colourful story.

Megabazus sent seven of the most prominent Persians in his army to the Macedonian court to demand submission. Amyntas, the aged king, agreed and invited the Persians to dinner. Both Macedonians and Persians had, in the ancient world, the name of being heavy drinkers and these Persians got very drunk at the drinking bout which followed the dinner proper. Becoming rowdy, they demanded that the Macedonians bring in their women to join the company. Although Amyntas pointed out that this was contrary to Macedonian custom, he had no choice but to obey. The women appeared and were put seated opposite the Persians. These soon began to complain, saying they were being titillated. The women then moved beside them. When the ambassadors began to paw them, this was too much for Amyntas' son Alexander, who conceived a plan. Bidding his father go to bed, he told his guests they could have any woman they liked, but should allow them first to go and clean up. To this the Persians agreed. Alexander then picked out some smooth cheeked young men, put them in women's dresses and gave them daggers. These entered the dining room and, when the envoys tried to molest them, stabbed them to death. Afterwards the Persians made great but vain efforts to find their missing officials, but Alexander managed to escape retribution by bribing the head of the search-party and giving him his own sister in marriage.

These last details reveal the story for what it almost certainly is, a concoction by Alexander, a man we shall be hearing some more of again. Persians were not in the habit of letting pass the disappearance of their own, especially when they had opportunity of visiting retribution on the man suspected of being implicated in it. And very few subjects married into that aristocracy let alone someone who was suspected of murder of one of their kind. The truth seems to be that not only had Alexander medized, that is to say he had thrown in his lot with the Persians, now and again when Mardonius came that way a little later, but he had profited greatly thereby. As we shall see, he was a somewhat slippery person and, when the defeat of Xerxes meant his position was subjected to scrutiny, he cleverly put about this fable to conceal what he had actually done.[12]

Megabazus was also given the job of dealing with the Paeonians who lived near the Hellespont. Here again there is a story worth telling since there is much history to learn from it. On his way back from Scythia, Darius rested at Sardis and there saw something remarkable. A good-looking girl, with a water pot on her head, led a horse by the bridle while spinning flax all the while. Coming to a river, she was observed to water the horse, fill the pot and still continue spinning. Darius ordered her into his presence. She was accompanied by her two brothers, who had arranged the whole scene to catch the king's attention. They told him where they were from and asked to be placed under his overlordship adding, in answer to a question from Darius, that many women in their country were like their sister.

This is the point at which a pretty tale becomes sinister. Greek states had a distinct tendency to split into factions. Moreover, when the Persians were about many of these did not hesitate to call them in, in order to get the better of their enemies. The principle was a simple one: having the Persians as masters was a price worth paying if you could thereby become a master yourself in your own city, and it is worth emphasising now that we shall meet with the phenomenon more than once in the course of the rest of this book.

In this instance, things did not fall out as the Paeonians had hoped, for it would seem their little charade was just too successful. Instead of placing them in power, Darius ordered Megabazus to transplant this industrious people to Asia. As he approached, the Paeonians gathered on the coastal road to block him but he slipped behind them and captured their towns. At this, resistance collapsed and the whole nation was carted off to Asia.[13]

At Sardis, too, Darius performed another task, the reward for service in the late campaign. If Coes really had given the advice he is supposed to have at the bridge, then he had his reward. From being a private citizen of Mytilene, he now became its tyrant. Histiaeus, also, had his work in preserving the bridge recognized. As he was already a tyrant, he asked for, and got, a place called Myrcinus in Thrace, where he intended to found a new city. As might be expected, the part Miltiades had played in events ensured a different fate was in store for him. At some point – the chronology is obscure – he was obliged to flee the Chersonese when the Persians came looking for him. In fact, his son was captured and he himself barely escaped the pursuing Persian navy. Returning to Athens he beat off a politically motivated prosecution and was, as we shall see eventually, to play a major part in Athenian public life.

Histiaeus did not long enjoy his rule in Thrace. On his campaigns there, Megabazus passed by Myrcinus and saw what he was about. Upon his return to Susa he, almost certainly with malicious intent, laid information against Histiaeus. He pointed out that he had much timber for ship building and ruled over a numerous population who were ready to obey him and who, if he started a war, could be paid from silver mines in the area. There was, he said, very real potential for Histiaeus to turn rebel. Darius took this seriously and summoned Histiaeus to court, saying that he still felt the need of such a wise councillor. Once he got him there, Darius bestowed great honours on him. He did make of him a royal councillor and gave him the even rarer privilege of dining at the royal table. But none of these marks of favour could disguise the fact that Histiaeus was now both idle and powerless and that Darius was resolved he should remain so. A restless, ambitious and industrious man, Histiaeus began to tire of his captivity. He resolved to get out of the Persian court but the device he hit upon was to lead to a great war.[14]

Chapter 2

The Ionian Revolt (499–494 BC)

One day in 500 BC, a group of oligarchic exiles from Naxos, rudely dubbed the Fat by the democratic faction which had expelled them, as they had grown sleek in their days in power, turned up in Miletus. They had come to wait upon its ruler Aristagoras. He was a nephew of Histiaeus and had charge of the city in his uncle's unavoidable absence in Susa. The Naxian request was a simple one, that he should restore them to power. Aristagoras seems to have been a man with an eye to the main chance. He saw here an opportunity to become ruler of the island and told the exiles he would see what he could do for them but that first he would have to have the permission of Artapharnes, satrap of Sardis, to mount an expedition. By lauding the amenities of the island he persuaded the satrap that an attack was worthwhile. The request then went up the chain of command to the royal court at Susa from where permission was duly granted.

A fleet of two hundred ships, manned by Persians and their subjects, was assembled and set sail. Aristagoras had overall command of the expedition but the soldiers on board were under the command of Megabates, a cousin of Darius. Out of this clumsy arrangement there came disaster to the expedition. One night, on one of the vessels Megabates found no watch was being kept and promptly jammed the ship's captain's head through an oar-hole. Aristagoras was summoned and used his authority to free the victim. This enraged Megabates who then sent a boat to warn the Naxians as to what was in store for them. Modern scholarly doubts about this story are needless. Persian nobles disliked Greek upstarts and, as an Achaemenid, Megabates could ill tolerate being ordered about from such a quarter. Moreover, as we shall see in a moment, he had nothing to fear if word of what he had done should get out. As for the Naxians, they gathered supplies and put their town in readiness for a siege. For four months the Persians assaulted it and then, with supplies failing, they were forced to pull out.[1]

Having botched the operation in this way, Aristagoras knew there would be trouble. He had squandered a good deal of Persian money and he would be blamed for alerting the Naxians. Megabates was, of course, culpable but he would present a fallacious account of events to Darius who, for all that he had certain phil-Hellene tendencies, would in this instance choose the word of a Persian before that of a Greek. As Aristagoras was pondering his dilemma there came to Miletus the man with the tattooed head.

Histiaeus, tiring of his luxurious captivity at the Persian court, calculated that if there was an uprising in Ionia, Darius would send him to suppress it. Guards on the roads, however, made sending a letter hazardous so, the story goes, he hit on an ingenious device. He shaved the head of a slave, tattooed the word 'revolt' on it and when the hair grew again sent him to Aristagoras. He, reading the message, summoned his supporters and called for an uprising. Only one voice was raised in dissent, that of the geographer Hecateus. He reminded his audience of the power of those they were proposing to take on. When this did not impress his audience he suggested they seize a temple treasure and use the money to achieve mastery of the sea. Again his listeners were not convinced and the revolt began. Aristagoras resigned his tyranny and all over Ionia his supporters turned on their tyrant rulers and drove them out. Thus began a revolution which, at its height, spread from Ionia to embrace the Hellespont, Cyprus and Caria, a non-Greek area where warriors wielded their native weapon, a double-headed axe, with deadly dexterity.[2]

Why Histiaeus and Aristagoras should want to rise up is clear enough. What is a matter of dispute is why so many others should want to follow this rackety pair in what, not to put too fine a point on it, was a hazardous enterprise. Plainly they were able to capitalize on widespread discontent but there is debate as to what exactly that discontent was. Modern historians, from time to time, complain that Herodotus has not quite got it right. Something more than a desire for a change in the system of government must be in question. So other motives are occasionally invoked, such as the economic. Persian rule had been deleterious to business in Ionia and the heavy tribute ensured a constant drain of specie which would never return. But this is, at base, mere guesswork and if we bear steadily in mind the lively interest Greeks ever showed in politics we can see that what Herodotus says is both consistent and plausible. When we first glimpsed discontent at the Danube bridge its object was not so much Persian rule as that of tyrants and the revolt now is the natural consequence of this. In the Greek homeland, tyranny, so common a generation or so before, had given way to a more broadly based form of government. It now had something of the archaic about it. Excited by new ideas, the Greeks of Asia could not see why they too should not share in the benefits they might confer.[3]

But now, in 499 BC, Aristagoras knew full well the probable consequences of his actions so he set off for the Greek homeland in a search for allies. He naturally made first for the strongest state, Sparta, and there had an interview with King Cleomenes. He brought with him a bronze tablet on which there was engraved some kind of primitive map of the Middle East. Waving this before the king, he showed him, if not all the kingdoms of the world, at least a reasonable selection. There is more than a suspicion that Aristagoras was of a naturally crooked temperament and that a native tendency to mendacity had been honed by years of dealing with his Persian masters. At any rate, he now told two outright lies. All of the peoples of Asia were rich and, in addition they were totally unwarlike. They were obvious targets for the Spartans. Why were they wasting time fighting over the poor lands of the Peloponnese with tough opponents like the Argives when, for no effort, they might have the riches of the East?

It does not seem to have occurred to Cleomenes to ask what we might: why if the natives of Asia were so useless in war, was Aristagoras looking for help against them? Instead the Spartan king asked a very Greek question. How far was it from the coast to Susa? For some reason Aristagoras now decided to tell the truth and in so doing ruined himself. It was, he said, a journey of three months. Cleomenes reacted by ordering him to leave Sparta by night fall. Speaking generally, Greeks were uneasy at being far from the sea but the Spartans had their own especial reasons for dislike of being far from home. In their absence the helots might become restless and enemies like the Argives would attempt to take advantage of the situation.

Aristagoras, however, was not yet ready to give up. Clad as a suppliant, he approached Cleomenes again and began to promise him large sums of money. Spartans had the reputation of being avaricious and Cleomenes proved to be no exception. He began to waver when his daughter, Gorgo, a horribly precocious nine year old, who was present, cried out, 'he'll corrupt you'. Upon this Cleomenes withdrew.[4]

So Aristagoras was forced to try his luck in Athens and Eretria. Appearing before the Athenian assembly he told his hearers more or less what he had told Cleomenes about Asia. The Athenians proved receptive. Traditionally they were believed to be ancestors of the Ionians who had migrated around 1000 BC and in addition they had their own quarrel to pursue with Persia. When, a few years before, in 507 BC, they had expelled their Pisistratid tyrant Hippias and established a democracy, they had found themselves surrounded by enemies. So they requested an alliance with the Persians. This they were ready to grant on condition the Athenians recognized their overlordship. But then there had come a change of sentiment and the Athenians repudiated the agreement. To compound the quarrel, Artaphernes had a little later sent a direct order that they should reinstate Hippias. In consequence Aristagoras obtained twenty five ships from the Athenians and five from Eretria. The expedition set off in 498 BC.[5]

The allies came ashore at Ephesus where they were joined by local forces. From here they marched up country, passed over Mount Tmolus and, coming to Sardis, captured the whole city except for the citadel where Artaphernes held out. Unfortunately there was now an accident. The city consisted of straw huts and when a fire started the entire place burned to the ground. In the conflagration a temple was destroyed and the Persians were to recall this act of sacrilege when they came looking for revenge. Now their forces were gathering and the Greek position became intolerable. So, with the Persians in pursuit, the allies retreated to the coast. In a battle fought at Ephesus the Persians emerged as victors. After this the Athenians and Eretrians returned home and refused all further Ionian requests for help.

This change of policy is as mysterious as the earlier repudiation of the sought after alliance with Persia by Athens, for no ancient author explains why it came about. The changeability of a democracy which now regretted this adventure may have had something to do with it and those who had earlier sought an accommodation with Persia may have once more become influential. What is beyond dispute is that Herodotus was right when he described the expedition as the beginning of great ills for Greeks and barbarians. Before we see why we must complete our narrative of the Ionian revolt and its aftermath.[6]

We now find the Persians counterattacking. In campaigns which modern authorities believe extended over the years 497–496 BC, they operated successfully in the Dardanelles, the region of the Sea of Marmara and the Troad before moving against Ionia itself. In Caria, too, the Persians advanced and defeated the Carians on the Marsyas River. The Milesians then came to aid their allies but together they were worsted in a second battle. The Carians, though, rallied sufficiently to destroy another Persian force in an ambush and it may be as late as 494 BC before they were completely conquered.

Meantime (496 BC) Cyprus had been re-conquered. A Persian force slipped past an Ionian fleet and, aided by treachery in the opposing ranks, defeated the Cypriots at a place called Salamis which should not, of course, be confused with the more famous place which was to witness a great Greek victory during Xerxes' invasion. A virtually simultaneous victory over the Persian fleet by the Ionian navy did nothing to retrieve the situation and a series of sieges brought resistance on the island to an end.[7]

By now Aristagoras seems to have begun to have doubts – well founded it is clear to us – that his revolt would turn out well. So he headed for Thrace intending to establish there some kind of refuge for the Ionians, should, as was becoming increasingly likely, they have need of it. Unfortunately the Thracians were none too keen on the idea and killed him as he was laying siege to one of their towns.[8]

By now, too, Histiaeus had arrived on the coast, having persuaded Darius, who did have his suspicions of his role in the affair, that he was blameless and that he could put an end to the revolt and even conquer Sardinia for him. Our sources sometimes depict Persians as being slower of wit than Greeks but in Artaphernes, if not in Darius, Histiaeus met his match. In what must have been an uncomfortable interview, the plain speaking satrap told him he knew the truth or, as he put it, Aristagoras had put on a shoe sewn by Histiaeus. Histiaeus took fright at this and fled to Chios. The Chians, at first, thought he really was a Persian agent but he managed to persuade them otherwise. From here he engaged in yet another intrigue, sending treacherous letters to disaffected members of the satrapal court at Sardis. These, though, were intercepted by Artaphernes and the recipients were duly executed.

By now, the Chians seem to have been anxious to be rid of their guest and so they shipped him to his old fief Miletus. The people there, however, had acquired a taste for liberty and would have nothing to do with their former ruler. So Histiaeus had to return to Chios. The Chians refused his request for ships but eventually prevailed upon the Lesbians to give him eight vessels. With these he made for Byzantium where he embarked on a career as a privateer.⁹

We are ill-informed about events in 495 BC but by the next year it becomes clear that only a few places held out on mainland Ionia and the Persians began preparations to move against Miletus, the chief centre of resistance, by land and sea. As their forces invested the landward side, the remaining Ionians – largely by now from the islands – gathered their fleet by the island of Lade, which lay off the town, for the decision had been made to concentrate on a defence by sea.

As they awaited the arrival of the Persian fleet, the Ionians appointed as an admiral a certain Dionysius from Phocea even though he had brought only three ships. It was not, perhaps, the wisest choice. Dionysius imposed strict discipline and made the crews practise all day under the hot Mediterranean sun. Eventually tempers shortened and people began to murmur against the strict regime and the highhandedness of one whose state contributed so little. The upshot was that the Ionians refused to serve Dionysius any further and elected instead to sulk in the cool of their tents.

When the Persians arrived with their fleet they set about sowing further dissension. They sent the deposed tyrants among the Ionians with a message. No harm would come to those who yielded now. Persistence would mean, on the other hand, enslavement of men, castration of boys and the shipment of young women to the harem. The Samians alone indicated they would comply.

When both sides lined up for battle, the Samians simply sailed away. This disheartened the Lesbians who were next to them and they too then sailed off. Of those who remained, the Chians gave a good account of themselves but to no avail for the Persians had won. They now pressed the siege of Miletus and eventually took it.

Soon after the storming and burning of the city, Histiaeus, hearing the news, sailed south from Byzantium. With a force of Lesbians he first attacked and subdued a Chian garrison. In the next year (443) he mounted an assault on Thasos. Hearing that the Persian fleet was now about the business of subduing the islands, he hurried to Lesbos and from there made his way to the mainland in search of provisions. Unfortunately he fell in with a Persian force which defeated him. He was brought to Artaphernes who had him executed and then sent his embalmed head to Darius. The satrap did this because he feared that if Histiaeus made it to Susa alive he would once more successfully charm Darius. As it turned out, Darius did mourn his loss and gave the head honourable burial as was fitting for one who had once done the Achaemenids great service.

After this the Persian fleet subdued Chios, Lesbos and Tenedos, and with this the Ionian revolt was at an end.[10]

But Darius was not finished with Ionia. He had played the conqueror, now he played the administrator. It was doubtless at his behest that Artaphernes summoned representatives from all the Ionian states and made them swear to settle any disputes which might arise among them by arbitration. The inveterately quarrelsome were required to renounce force and have recourse to judicial procedures. Further he carried out a survey of their lands and on this basis fixed the tribute. But there was more to come.

In the next year (492 BC) there arrived on the coast a new supreme commander. He was Mardonius, son-in-law of Darius and one of the coming men at the Persian court. He had with him an army and a fleet. When he got to Cilicia he handed his army over to subordinates to take to the Hellespont. He himself sailed along the coast to Ionia where he did something which amazed the Greeks. He abolished the tyrannies and put democracies in their place. He then made for the Hellespont and shipped his army over. The operation then became two-pronged. The fleet subdued Thasos and then sailed to Acanthus. Off the promontory of Mount Athos they were caught in a great storm in which many lives and ships were lost. Many men were actually devoured by vicious fish of a type unspecified in our sources. Meantime, on land, Mardonius completed the subjugation of Macedonia begun by Megabazus. Among the Thracians he was not quite so fortunate. A tribe called the Brygi attacked his camp one night, inflicting heavy casualties and wounding Mardonius himself. He did not give up and remained until he had conquered them. Then he returned to Asia.[11]

The Ionian revolt can be seen to have three consequences. In the first place it moved Darius, who ever sought good order in his dominions, to make changes in the way Ionia was governed. The Greeks of that region had now got the kind of regime they wanted but whether they were happy at the price they had had to pay is a moot point. In the second instance, it is plain that Darius had been encouraged to widen his conquests and round off the borders of his dominions by taking in the northern regions of the Greek homeland. The third consequence is from our point of view the most important. Hitherto communication between the Greek homeland and Persia had been on the diplomatic level. Such exchanges had been sporadic and, if hardly cordial, had not been violent. Now all that was changed. The Athenians and Eretrians had challenged the King of Persia, invaded his lands and came into direct collision with his armies.

Years before, when the Spartans had provoked him, Cyrus had asked who these people were. Now, on hearing of the burning of Sardis, Darius asked the same question about the Athenians and, as Cyrus had done in his day, determined to give them some troubles of their own. He took his bow, the drawing of which showed his strength and shot an arrow praying, as he did so, that it would be granted to him to take his revenge on them. And to make sure the matter would not slip his mind, he commanded a slave every time dinner was served to repeat three times, 'remember, o king, the Athenians'.[12]

Chapter 3

Marathon (490 BC)

Now that the frontier of the empire was contiguous with Thessaly, Darius was ready to give his full attention to Athens and Eretria. He had at court the exiled Pisistratids who had been banished by the new democratic regime in Athens. They seem to have been making nuisances of themselves, constantly badgering their host to restore them to what they regarded their rightful position. It would be rash to deny this had no effect on the king but it would be even rasher to claim it was his main motive for moving against these enemies. The man who asked to be constantly reminded of the Athenians sought revenge for the damage they had done. As a follower of Ahura Mazda, Darius ever sought balance. An evil deed must receive just retribution.

So, in 491 BC, Darius sent messengers to the mainland and the islands to demand earth and water. This gesture may call for a word of explanation. The Persians conceived of the world as being in the shape of an egg. The upper half was composed of air. Then came the earth and below it the waters. Now, what Darius sought was clear enough. No man controls the air but the yielding of earth and water symbolized Persian overlordship of these elements. Many on the mainland and the islands, rightly fearing the power of the Achaemenids, gave the asked for tokens. However, from the Persian point of view, the response from Athens and Sparta was disappointing since the request met with a refusal. At Athens the messengers were tossed into a pit into which condemned criminals were thrown. At Sparta they were chucked into a well and told to get their earth and water there.

This violation of the sacrosanctity of ambassadors constituted, in ancient belief, a sacrilege. We hear of no ill-consequences for the Athenians but divine wrath, we are assured, followed the Spartans for their impious act. For a long time they could get no favourable omens at sacrifice. Eventually they sent two men to Darius' son Xerxes to offer their lives in reparation for what had been done. On the road this pair had the hardihood to read a lecture on freedom to a satrap they encountered but when they got to Susa they met their match. Xerxes disdained to harm them lest he himself become, in turn, a party to impiety and simply sent them home.[1]

While the messengers were about their business, Darius, rightly assuming that not all Greeks would be co-operative, began making preparations for the expedition. There was to be a change of strategy. We are rather ill-informed on how decisions were actually reached at the Persian court. We are not privy to the private thoughts of the king. No private letters or memoranda survive. All that we have from the Persian side are some inscriptions which, in the main, extol the virtues and qualities of the monarch or list his conquests. From the Greek side, we catch, from Herodotus, glimpses of discussion at court but that is all. Nevertheless, we can be sure that the decision to set the expedition afoot and the manner in which it was to be conducted originated with Darius himself. An autocrat in an autocratic society, only he could mount an operation of such magnitude.

The change in strategy was radical. With Mardonius recovering from his wound and possibly out of regal favour, his combined land and sea operations were abandoned. Instead it was decided the whole armament would be taken in ships by way of the Cyclades. A new commander, too, was appointed: Datis, a Mede who was to be accompanied by Artaphernes, a nephew of the king. The number of the fleet is given as six hundred and this comprised both warships and vessels specially adapted to carry horses. We are not given specific details of the modifications for the animals but one thing is clear: the Persians intended to deploy to the full their strongest arm. There is some reason, however, to believe the size of the fleet may be exaggerated and it is, in fact, doubtful if, at this point anyway, Darius was aiming at the subjugation of the whole of Greece. Rather his aim was the settling of scores with Athens and Eretria.

The land troops made their way to Cilicia. Here they joined up with the fleet. The force then made its way to Samos and from here to Naxos. The failure to subdue this island in the expedition of Aristagoras had not been forgotten and an assault was duly mounted. The Naxians, for their part, took to the hills. The Persians caught some of them and made slaves of them. They then burned the city to the ground.

The Delians, knowing they were next, also fled but then received a surprise. Datis sent them a message telling them he would do them no harm. The island was sacred to Apollo and he reminded his audience that this was a god who had always been revered by the Persians. Encouraged, the people returned to their homes and, instead of burning the town, the Persians burnt a rich offering on the altar of the god. They then sailed away but by now they had thoroughly frightened the other islands and so the rest of the Cyclades yielded to them.[2]

In Euboea the Persians came ashore in the south at the town of Carystus. The townsfolk refused to give hostages or supply troops to the Persians. The latter, however, laid siege to the town and ravaged the countryside so that the Carystians were eventually forced to yield. The Persians then advanced against Eretria itself. The Eretrians appealed to Athens for help and she despatched to them four thousand cleruchs or settlers who had estates in Chalcidice. These, however, soon discovered there was a strong pro-Persian faction in the town and were warned by one Aischines of the disaster which was likely to befall. So the Athenians pulled out and crossed the Euripus channel to safety.

The Eretrians would not meet the Persians in the open but took shelter behind their walls. An assault, which lasted six days, was mounted and many were killed on both sides. Then, on the seventh day, the town was betrayed, its temples burned and its people reduced to slavery. The fears of the Athenians and, we may say, the expectations of the enemy had been amply fulfilled for this was not the first time the Persians had had experience of the ruinous factionalism in Greek states.[3]

With the Eretrians disposed of it was now the turn of Athens. The city was not directly attacked. Instead the Persians put in at Marathon, a plain some twenty six miles from Athens. The choice was both strategic and political. The curving bay provided anchorage for ships and the plain was suitable for cavalry who could graze their horses on the edge of a marsh which lay behind the Persian lines. The political becomes explicable when we learn that Hippias, the exiled Pisistratid tyrant who had evidently successfully worked on Darius, was travelling in the entourage of Datis.

His presence shows plainly that Darius had something different in mind for Athens from what he had just meted out to the Eretrians. His design was the restoration of the Pisistratid tyranny. Nor would Hippias be a mere figurehead or man of straw. We have learnt enough now of the Persians to realize they had long been accustomed to allow a great deal of latitude to their underlings, provided those underlings acknowledged the suzerainty of their overlords. For their part, these same underlings were happy with such an arrangement since it allowed them to dominate their fellow citizens. Hippias could, once more, wield real power. Nor did his chances of recovery of that power seem faint. It was no secret that he had supporters still in Athens and that anyway there were also those who were simply doubtful of an Athenian victory. The supporters were eventually to reveal themselves but for now Marathon was the place to be. From here, long ago, his father Pisistratus had launched his own successful return from exile and here too Hippias could still count on support for his cause.

The omens, however, were unfavourable – in a literal sense. In one of those stories which enliven ancient historiography, we are told Hippias had dreamt he had had sex with his mother, which he interpreted as meaning he would yet lie in his native land. But, coming ashore, he coughed out a tooth and no amount of searching could find it. In many such stories we are informed an ancient did not understand a sign thus vouchsafed. Hippias, though, was no Macbeth to dismiss the notion that Birnam wood would come to Dunsinane. He correctly deduced he would leave nothing of himself in Attica except for that tooth.[4]

Democracy favours the disputatious and fosters debate. So now there was dispute and debate in Athens. Should the Athenians remain behind their walls or go forth to meet the Persians? Given that there was still a pro-Pisistratid element in the town, the recent events at Eretria counselled against lurking behind a barrier. Miltiades, who was now a powerful figure in Athenian politics, favoured an aggressive stance. So it was decided to march and the Athenian army proceeded along the main road to Marathon, which lies to the east of Mount Pentelicus.

Arriving on the plain they took up position on the southern side of the plain at a shrine to Hercules. From here they were able to block not only the road by which they had come but also a rough track over the mountain. This was necessary for, as we shall see when we come to speak of Thermopylae, the Persians were skilled in mountain warfare and could have exploited this route. It is also believed that they further strengthened their position by cutting down some trees and using them to form a kind of crude barricade.

Soon the Athenians were joined by a contingent from the small town of Plataea. Some years before, the Plataeans, threatened by Thebes, had applied to Sparta for help. The Spartans said they were too far off to be of use and referred them to the Athenians who duly took them under their protection. The Plataean gesture now was never forgotten and ever after at the Great Panatheneia the Athenians prayed not only for their own welfare but also that of the Plataeans.

But help was also sought from a more powerful state, Sparta. A professional runner named Pheidippides was despatched there to ask for aid. He made the journey in a day but afterwards reported that he had had a vision of Pan on the way. The god had upbraided the Athenians for their neglect of him when he had always been favourable to them. Some moderns think his exertions may have caused Pheidippides to hallucinate but his contemporaries took the matter seriously and, when the wars were done, built a shrine to Pan beneath the Acropolis. So far as the Spartans were concerned, they said they were willing but added they could not move immediately since they were celebrating a religious festival. It was the ninth day of the month and a taboo forbade their moving until the moon was full. To dismiss this as a piece of superstition or, worse, an exercise in cynicism would be to mistake its significance. Religious belief counted for much in Ancient Greece and this refusal of the Spartans to bestir themselves immediately was grounded in such a belief.

For several days the Athenians and Persians continued to face each other without either side making a move. The Athenians were awaiting the arrival of the Spartans while the Persians were still expecting their supporters in Athens to make a move.

Herodotus says the Athenians had ten generals and that opinion among them was equally divided on giving battle: five were for, five against. In addition there was a Polemarch, Callimachus, appointed by lot, who also had a vote. Miltiades went to work on him, pointing out that yielding to Persia would mean having Hippias back. He urged fighting before the disagreement in the high command became actual dissension. Callimachus was persuaded and gave his vote for action. Each general presided for a day but those who had voted to attack, when their turn came, resigned their authority to Miltiades. He preferred though to wait until his own day to hold command came round. It should be noted, though, that not all scholars accept this version of events and think Herodotus may have mistaken the role of the Polemarch and believe he actually held supreme command and that it was he who took the final decision. Nevertheless, irrespective of which version we elect to follow, it is generally agreed that Miltiades played a prominent part

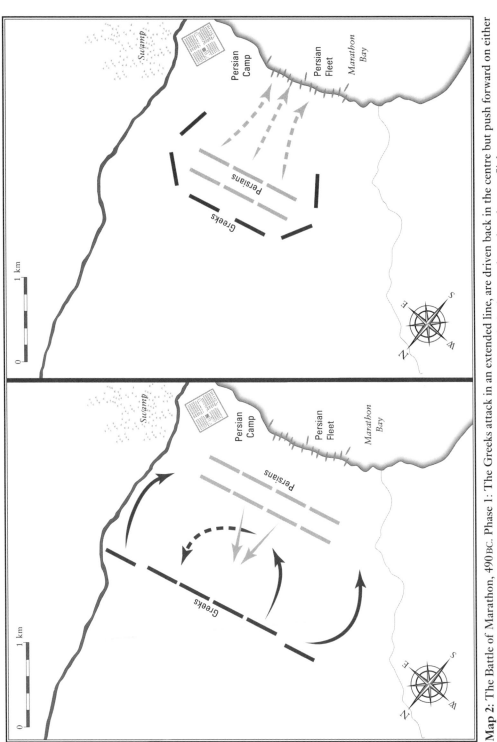

Map 2: The Battle of Marathon, 490 BC. Phase 1: The Greeks attack in an extended line, are driven back in the centre but push forward on either flank. Phase 2: The Greek wings turn in on the Persian centre, threatening to encircle them and putting them to flight.

in determining tactics and that much of the credit for the subsequent victory must be given to him.[5]

Battle at last was joined but when it comes it brings with it a puzzle for the modern historian. We have made great play of the fact that the Persians had arrived equipped for and ready to fight a cavalry battle. Yet Herodotus, our chief source, says nothing about their participation. They are absent from his account. The only clue as to what had happened is supplied by a late source called the Suda, an encyclopaedia compiled in Byzantine times. This preserves a notice which says that some Ionians, impressed into Persian service, had sneaked across to the Athenian line and, at the wooden barricade which it will be remembered had been erected there, told the Athenians that the Persian cavalry was withdrawing. Datis, it seems, had grown tired of waiting for his putative allies and decided to re-embark and sail around behind the enemy lines in order to attack Athens. To cover this manoeuvre the bulk of the Persian forces were moved closer to the Athenian positions.[6]

The Athenians, on being informed of what was going on, advanced. They were obliged to extend their line of battle considerably in order to cover the whole of the enemy front. The result was that their centre was weak, being only a few lines deep. The wings, on the other hand, were strong. Conventional wisdom holds that hoplites usually fought in tight formation but these men fanned out and advanced at speed across the broken ground of the plain. The aim was to prevent the Persians from making full use of their archers. The Persians themselves were amazed not just by the tactic but by the boldness thus displayed. Their past experience of Greeks had not prepared them for something like this.

The Persians themselves and their formidable subjects, the Sacae, were in the centre and they there prevailed against the Greeks, chasing them inland. On the wings the Athenians and Plataeans got the upper hand. Leaving those they had defeated where they were, the two wings then turned against the Persian centre. There occurred the greatest slaughter of the enemy as some perished at the hands of the Greeks or drowned in the nearby swamps as they tried to flee. Those on the flanks were luckier. As we saw, they had been left by the Athenians and many were able to take advantage of this circumstance and make their way to the ships. By the time the Athenians had chased the remnant of the defeated Persian centre to the shore, they found they were too late. The bulk of the fleet, with many of the aforementioned refugees from the Persian wings, had put out to sea and the Athenians were only able to seize seven vessels.

Ancient battle statistics are generally believed to be, at best, intelligent guesses but the figures for this particular encounter are usually held to be reasonably accurate. Over six thousand Persians lost their lives while 192 Athenians fell. Among these was the Polemarch Callimachus, who held the right wing, the place of honour, and perished in the final assault on the ships.[7]

Later tradition records how the good news was brought from Marathon to Athens. According to this account, Pheidippides, he who had gone to Sparta to look for help, now ran back to town. Bursting into the agora, he gasped out the news and then dropped dead. Although this provides the inspiration for the modern marathon race, it is unlikely to be true. Not only is the source tradition suspect but it was the Athenian army itself which brought news of the victory.[8]

Just as the Persian ships were pulling away, Hippias' supporters at last made their move. From a height – probably that of Pentelicus – a signal was given by the flashing of a shield which captured the strong Mediterranean sun. To this day, two questions remain unanswered. First of all, it is not known who did the deed. At the time suspicion fell on the family of the Alcmaeonidae who were opponents of Miltiades and who, conceivably, might, like many other Greeks, have been willing to accept Persian hegemony in return for dominance over domestic enemies. Herodotus spends some time defending the family from the charge and the case must surely be marked as 'not proven'. The second puzzle is what the signal meant to convey. Did it mean the medizers were now ready to rise or, in the light of the defeat, that now they were not? Again we must confess ignorance. What we do know is that when the Persians arrived at Phaleron, then port of Athens, the Athenian army was already waiting and, after a few days, Datis sailed away back to Asia.

On the way he had a dream which prompted him to search the fleet thoroughly. In a Phoenician ship he found a statue of Apollo which had been stolen during a reconnaissance. He personally took this to Delos and instructed the islanders to return it to its rightful place, Delium in Theban territory, but this was not done until some years later. After this Datis came to Susa to make his report. It was not unknown for Darius to visit impalement or other unpleasant punishments on those who crossed him. In the present instance his mood was benign. Although he had the Eretrian captives he did them no harm but settled them nearby where they long maintained their own individual Greek identity.

Meanwhile back at Marathon the Spartans arrived on the day after the battle. They inspected the dead, congratulated the Athenians and headed back home.[9]

Marathon quickly achieved revered status. In later antiquity the battlefield was believed to be haunted. By night you could hear the sound of horses and of men doing battle. Ill, it was said, befell you if you lingered to take a closer look but no harm came to anybody who stumbled on the scene by accident and reverence continues to the present day. Enclosed within a park may be seen the Soros or mound which is thought to contain the bodies of the Athenian dead.[10]

Chapter 4

Between the Invasions (489–481 BC)

Immediately after the reverse at Marathon, Darius began preparations for another assault on Greece. This army was to be even greater than before. For three years Asia Minor was ransacked for men and supplies and, so the Greeks believed, the whole place was in turmoil. Here a word of warning will be in order. Greeks were always wont to magnify their own importance to, and influence on, the king of Persia. We, on the other hand, can assume a more measured perspective and see that, in the vast Persian empire, the Greeks were only one of many concerns and not the greatest.

Then came an interruption. Egypt revolted. This was one of the richest – if not the richest – provinces in the empire, but also one of the most disaffected. For a large part of the fourth century BC it was to mount a successful rebellion and remain out of royal control. Now, however, one campaign was sufficient to crush the uprising. The crushing was not done by Darius, for he died in November 486 BC to be succeeded by his son Xerxes. Darius had sons born to him before he became king but he passed over these in favour of Xerxes, who was his first born after he ascended to the throne. We believe the report that Xerxes' mother Atossa had something to do with it, but not the foolish tale that a Spartan king called Demaratus, who was a refugee at the Persian court, having fallen foul of Cleomenes, had advised Darius to act thus. Persian kings were not in the habit of taking advice from refugees and what we have here is a splendid example of that Greek tendency to exaggerate their own importance in Persian circles, to which we alluded earlier.[1]

When he came to the throne, Xerxes was in his early thirties. He was said to have been tall and handsome and kingly in his appearance and manner. He could be capable of great acts of chivalry but also of great acts of cruelty. He was especially noted for his uncertain temper. Like a petulant adolescent, he was prone to rages which sometimes made him a danger to those around him. This much may be regarded as objective but three other grounds have been put forward to form a more subjective judgement of innate weakness, which it may be maintained is not justified. In the first place, it is held against Xerxes that his expedition to Greece failed but we should never forget that so did that of Darius against Scythia and this in no way takes from his repute. Again, it is claimed one of Xerxes' actions on his expedition bordered on the crazy but, as we shall see in due course, his actions are perfectly consistent with Persian religious belief and practice. Finally, one of his amours is said to betoken a fundamental weakness of character. Xerxes is said to have fallen in love with the wife of his brother Masistes. When she would not yield he transferred his attention to her daughter Artaÿnte with more success. She, however, one day asked for a cloak Xerxes was wearing which had been woven by his wife Amestris. He reluctantly gave it but Amestris, discovering what had happened, contrived to have him hand over the girl's mother to her, whom she then proceeded to mutilate. At that Masistes attempted to revolt but Xerxes was able to forestall him. This, it may be conceded, is not a particularly edifying tale but it should be pointed out that antics in the bedroom do not necessarily interfere with the business of ruling. There will, one fears, always be dispute about Xerxes' character and capabilities but it may not be too wide of the mark to suggest that, while he was not negligible, he does not impress in the way that Darius, and even more, Cyrus do.[2]

Preparations for the Greek invasion appear to have been continuing while Egypt was being subdued. Xerxes was being urged from two quarters. The Pisistratids had not given up and told him they had a store of oracles which said he would succeed. Mardonius, now restored to health and favour, went about declaring Europe was a fertile place and full of trees – a prospect attractive to any Zoroastrian. Eventually Xerxes called a conference of leading courtiers to make a final decision.

Xerxes told his audience that he had something to live up to. A Persian king was expected to show himself a great warrior and he proposed to emulate the feats of his predecessors. In the present instance there was a further motive: scores had not yet been settled with those who had burnt the temples of Sardis. Mardonius then spoke. The Greeks, he said, were worthless as warriors. Those of Asia they had subdued long ago and he himself could testify from his own experience that those of the homeland were no better. Next up was Artabanus who, as he had with Darius on his Scythian expedition, croaked a warning. One had only to point to Darius to appreciate the dangers of such foreign adventures. The Greeks were far better fighters than Mardonius made them out to be. Nobody present would have forgotten Marathon. At this Xerxes flew into one of his rages. He declared that he would have his revenge for Sardis. Only the fact that Artabanus was his uncle saved him from a worse fate but, as it was, he would remain at home with the women. To some of us this might seem a more attractive prospect than the alternative which was currently being discussed, but for a Persian it was the greatest insult which could be offered, for in that macho society women were the weaker and inferior sex.

As he lay in bed that night, Xerxes began to have doubts. What looks so attractive at 6pm may wear a far different aspect at 3am. He resolved, therefore, to abandon the expedition only to have a phantom appear to him in a dream and warn him he must not. Xerxes elected to ignore this and in the morning apologized to Artabanus and told the courtiers there would be no attack on Greece. The next night, however, the phantom appeared again and told him to go to war or be prepared to lose the throne.

In the morning Xerxes sent for Artabanus and told him of the new visitation. To test its veracity he proposed Artabanus should don his clothes and sleep in his bed, since the Persians believed that if you donned a man's clothes you became that man. Artabanus, who was a prosy bore, read Xerxes another lecture on the nature of dreams and the necessity to choose the better way, before consenting. He, too, was visited by the phantom who made threats against him for trying to dissuade Xerxes from his course. Artabanus reported this to Xerxes and said he, too, now favoured the expedition. In this way, all dithering came to an end and war was resolved on. The story as we have told it may have been embellished and dramatized but, at base, it reveals two things: there was a difference of opinion in the higher echelons of Persia about whether an attack should be made on Greece and some saw, thanks to their experiences when serving Darius, that it could end in failure.[3]

The strategy to be followed now changed yet again from that of Darius. Xerxes reverted to the combined operations of Mardonius' previous expedition and it is a moot point how far the latter was responsible for this. Certainly he had, as we have just seen, been one of the foremost advocates of invasion and his part in it was to be prominent up until its end.

So, fleet and army would work together. There can be little doubt that Xerxes had put together a great armament but we have great difficulty in forming an exact, or even approximate, estimate of just how great it was. To start with the fleet. Our Greek sources put the number of ships at 1,207 precisely but all modern authorities agree that this is an undoubted exaggeration and it has been suggested that about half that number, six hundred, may be more likely.

A similar problem is encountered with the land army. Xerxes himself knew how many fighting men he had. On one of the halts on his march, he had ten thousand men packed together and then drew a circle round them. A fence was then constructed on the circle and, in turn, all the rest of the soldiers were marched into the area. Unfortunately what was clear to Xerxes then is hidden from us now. We are at the mercy of our Greek sources here too and they put the numbers at almost two million. This is simply impossible, as it would be beyond the capacity of even the most sophisticated and advanced modern countries to put such numbers into the field. Once more we are encountering the Greek tendency to exaggerate and, as they won, they were anxious to demonstrate the unequal odds they had faced and the great numbers they had had to overcome. Here again modern scholarship has been at work and a figure of around 200,000 has been proposed. This is more likely to be closer to the truth but it should be emphasized that it is still a paper figure and an approximation.

Inflation of numbers may, in fact, have begun early indeed. In 481 the Greeks, aware that something was happening, sent spies to report on Xerxes' army. They were caught, tortured and about to be put to death when the king intervened personally and had them released. He then ordered that they be shown everything before being sent home. Xerxes had every reason to display and none to conceal. Technology was primitive and the Persians had not recently made any great advances in the art of warfare. Then, as on a later occasion, an Eastern ruler was not deploying weapons of mass destruction. On the other hand, when the Greek agents reported the numbers and hopefully magnified them, it would thoroughly frighten and perhaps persuade some, at least, of their fellow countrymen to yield.[4]

Persians, naturally, formed the core of Xerxes' army and he brought with him most of his household together with the nobles of the court. But all of the nations of the empire were required to serve as well. The principle involved was a simple one: when the king and all around him went to war, everybody else went to war with them. A levy was strictly enforced, as a certain rich Lydian called Pythius found out. Possessor of a large fortune, he offered Xerxes a great gift. Xerxes was pleased and asked what he might give in return. Pythius, who seems to have been in ignorance of what had happened when a similar request was made of Darius, asked to be allowed to keep one of his sons at home. Enraged by the request, Xerxes said he would indeed grant what he had been asked. He then had the boy chopped in half and made his army march between the bits.

Herodotus says 46 nations made up Xerxes' army. These he lists and describes their weapons and armour. Obviously we cannot reproduce the whole list here but I propose to give a few samples before going on to pass some comments on it as a whole.

From the east of the empire there came the Bactrians with their felt caps, cane bows and short spears. From the same quarter came the Indians who wore cotton and also carried cane bows. The south was represented by, among others, the Arabs who had long bows. The Ethiopians, too, carried long bows with which they shot arrows tipped with stone. They were dressed in leopard and lion skins and also carried spears tipped with antelope horn, as well as knotted clubs. The Libyans, in turn, carried javelins hardened with fire and wore leather. The Paphlagonians of Asia Minor had wicker helmets, small shields, short spears, javelins and daggers.

Hopefully, even this abbreviated list will give some indication of the variety of peoples in, and the geographical extent of, the Achaemenid empire. Where exactly Herodotus got his information from is a matter for conjecture, but one theory which has a certain plausibility is that he had got hold of some kind of register of peoples kept by the Persians, who would need to know who they ruled over and who, in times of war, they might summon to the levy. A further problem now arises. Neither those peoples I have described, nor most of the others in Herodotus' list, were really equipped to face the heavily armed Greek hoplite, and we hear next to nothing of their taking part in the fighting. That was largely carried out by the Persians, with their cavalry and infantry who wore mail, carried wicker shields, spears and bows; the Medes who were similarly equipped and the Sacae, a Scythian people who carried bows, daggers and battle axes. This situation may be accounted for in one of two ways. It may very well be that only a token contingent of those whose usefulness would be small was actually called out to answer the levy. Another explanation which is sometimes given is that these peoples were indeed present in great numbers not to do much fighting but for show. The Achaemenids, were not averse to redundant display if it could impress and awake awe.

So far as the fleet is concerned, it must be borne in mind that the Persians, like the Romans after them, were essentially a land power and were never entirely comfortable on the sea. So, in this instance, we may believe reports that the ships were manned chiefly by Greeks and non-Greeks from Asia Minor, Phoenicians and Egyptians. These subject peoples did not do the actual fighting. Significantly, in view of what we said above about their role on land, Medes, Persians and Sacae were aboard the ships as marines.[5]

The most careful preparations were made to make smooth the path of the great army. It was determined that the fleet should not suffer round Mount Athos as it had during Mardonius' expedition, so three years were spent in digging a canal through the peninsula. Later, as the army was actually on the march, a road was constructed in Thrace. Used as they were to rough cart tracks and the like, this became an object of wonder to the local inhabitants. It was also regarded as a kind of gift, for, ever afterwards, they carefully maintained it. Bridges, too, figured prominently in these preparations. Those who dug around Mount Athos also had to bridge the Strymon River. However, the most famous were those thrown over the Hellespont to facilitate the movement of the army from Asia Minor to Europe.

There were, in fact, two such bridges built by the Phoenicians and secured by flax and papyrus cables. Unfortunately these were destroyed in a storm. Xerxes flew into one of his rages and had the engineers decapitated. A second pair of bridges, supported by boats, was then constructed and these held. What attracted most attention, though, was Xerxes' behaviour when he got to the Hellespont. He had it lashed and branded and threw fetters into it. To the Greeks this betokened overwhelming pride and impiety. At first glance it might seem to us to indicate mere childishness. But, from the Persian perspective, there was nothing untoward here. Saltwater was fresh water which had been tainted by the Evil Principle Ahriman, and so Xerxes was perfectly justified in assaulting it in this fashion. It is worth adding that, when Cyrus had behaved in a similar fashion, nobody had remarked on it but, once Xerxes had acquired a name for being erratic, many of his actions tended to be interpreted in the light of this judgement.

Food and drink for the men had also to be attended to. Water, it would seem, was not regarded as a problem, as that would be provided by rivers on the way. We may note in parenthesis that stories of these being drunk dry can be dismissed as yet another example of the exaggerations which attach to the estimate of the army's size. Food would come from two sources. Along the planned path through Macedonia and Thrace, dumps of supplies were established in advance of the army's arrival. Requisitioning was also resorted to. Towns in the army's path received, well in advance, precise instructions to bake bread and fatten fowl and cattle. Gold and silver tableware, as well as a special tent, had to be prepared for Xerxes. The Persians only ate one meal but the hardship involved for many of the towns can be easily imagined. The situation allowed a man of Abydus, Megacreon, to earn a reputation as a wit. He urged his fellow citizens to go to the temples and beg the gods in future to send only half the evils they had in store for them. Had Xerxes looked for two meals, they would all assuredly have been ruined.

As his preparations neared completion in 481 BC, Xerxes sent messengers to the states of Greece to demand earth and water, the tokens of surrender. Athens and Sparta alone were excepted, as Xerxes had not forgotten the treatment they had accorded to his father's emissaries. The reaction to this demand will be narrated after we have spoken of what the Greeks had been doing in this intervening period.[6]

At Athens the hero of Marathon had soon come to grief. In the following year (489 BC), Miltiades had asked for and obtained a fleet from the Athenians. He did not say where he was going but promised there would be profits. His target was actually Paros. The island had yielded to Datis and sent a ship to Marathon. This was the public reason given for the attack but it was also said Miltiades had a private grudge. One of the Parians had earlier slandered him to a Persian noble. The assault was not a success, as the Parians resolutely defended their walls. Baffled, Miltiades, following the advice of a local priestess, entered a shrine of Demeter near the town. What he hoped to achieve by this is not clear but, on the way out, he injured his leg climbing the wall of the shrine. Eventually there was nothing for it but to call off the operation and return profitless to Athens. There his enemies pounced and he was put on trial for fraud. His services to the state ensured he avoided a death sentence but he was fined heavily. For him, though, this mattered little. Miltiades' wound had turned gangrenous and he died shortly afterwards.[7]

But now a new figure came to the fore at Athens: Themistocles. Rumoured to have had a Thracian for a mother, he was, and would always be, something of an outsider. Yet, if the Athenians thought themselves to be the cleverest of the Greeks, then Themistocles had some claim to be the cleverest of the lot. Foresighted, supple and adaptable, he now beat off opponents such as Aristides the Just to become the most prominent man in the public life of the day. The qualities he now displayed were to be shown again in 480 BC so that he may, with some justification, be called, as Carnot was to be in Revolutionary France, 'the architect of the victory'. Even when the Athenians later turned against him, as they did with Miltiades, Themistocles was able to prevail upon the King of Persia, to whom, as we shall see, he was to do so much damage, to give him a place of refuge in his dominions.

During the 480s BC, many in Athens believed that the Persians had been taught a lesson at Marathon and would never return. Themistocles thought otherwise and determined the city should be ready. The Athenians possessed silver mines at Laurium and, at some time in the decade, a new vein was discovered. The initial proposal was to distribute the money as a bounty to every citizen. Themistocles, foreseeing how a fleet would be required should the Persians return, prevailed upon the people to build ships instead. In making his initial suggestion, he was aided by the fact that more ships would anyway be needed for the contemporary war with Aegina.

Aegina and Athens had long been rivals, but for us this only acquires significance at the time of Marathon because then the Aeginetans had been among those who had given earth and water. The dangers to Athens from this act of a near neighbour do not need to be emphasized. Help came to the Athenians from an unexpected quarter, Cleomenes of Sparta. We know from the reception he gave Aristagoras that he, like most of the rest of the Spartans, was opposed to foreign adventures but, with the Persians approaching the Greek homeland, he recognized the peril in which she stood and realized it was time to act. So he crossed over to the island to extract hostages for its good behaviour. He found himself successfully defied by the chief medizer, a man called Crius (Ram). As he departed in anger Cleomenes, playing on the name, told his opponent to gild his horns as was customary for a sacrificial victim because trouble was coming. Cleomenes kept his word and soon returned with the other Spartan king Leotychides. This time there was no resistance, and Crius and his friends were carted off to be held as hostages in Athens.

Shortly after Marathon, Cleomenes died and the Aeginetans made application to Sparta for the return of the hostages. The Spartans were willing but the Athenians refused to budge. In retaliation the Aeginetans seized an Athenian state ship and took the dignitaries on it hostage. Next the Athenians gave their backing to a democratic coup on the island, but delay in putting their fleet together meant they arrived too late and a great number of the insurgents were slaughtered. When the Athenians did eventually arrive they defeated the Aeginetans in a sea battle. The latter then sought the help of Argos and a body of volunteers duly appeared. Most of these perished in Aegina but the islanders subsequently inflicted a defeat on the Athenian navy. Details of subsequent clashes, if any, are not available to us but we do know the two states were still at war in 481 BC.[8]

By 481 BC the king had begun his march from Susa and this, with the demand for earth and water, made it clear to even the most dim-witted what lay in store for Greece. In the autumn of the year then those states who had determined on resistance came together at the Isthmus of Corinth. There they formed a league after swearing loyalty to each other. Agreement on one point was easy. These congenitally quarrelsome states recognized they would have to cease their internecine wars, the most serious of which was that between Athens and Aegina, which we have just been describing. Although there were to be stirrings of discontent on the issue on at least one subsequent occasion, it was agreed now that Sparta should have overall command of the league forces. Next, it was resolved to tithe all of those who voluntarily took the Persian side. The tenth of their property thus confiscated was to be dedicated at Delphi.[9]

Finally it was decided to try and broaden the league and invite other Greek states to come and assist in the common defence. Argos was now approached. From the first her response was coloured by her long standing enmity with Sparta, with whom she had contested the supremacy in the Peloponnese. A recent defeat at the hands of Cleomenes had not helped matters. When the delegates arrived, the Argives told them that they had been warned by an oracle to keep out of the war. Nevertheless they said they were prepared to take a risk and ignore this warning if two conditions were met: Sparta was to grant them a thirty year truce and they themselves were given the supreme command. The Spartans said they would think about the truce but the command was out of the question. The Argive reply to this was to order the delegates from their lands. In this way, then, the Argives medized but it is noteworthy that another story was circulating now and later. In this Xerxes himself sent a message to the Argives, telling them to remain neutral. They were, he said, relations because they both descended from a common ancestor, Perses, and thus they should not fight each other.[10]

A delegation also waited upon Gelon, tyrant of Syracuse. The Greeks in their diaspora had gone west as well as east, and there were many rich Greek cities in Sicily and southern Italy. Here, as in Ionia, there were still tyrants and the phenomenon lasted well into the fourth century due to the fact that the Greeks contested mastery of Sicily with the Carthaginians, who had settled here from their home, Carthage in North Africa. Defence against this Semitic people required strong and ruthless rulers. Gelon was one of those. He presided over a magnificent court in the powerful city of Syracuse.

It was natural the league should approach such a man, who had both an army and a fleet at his disposal. The interview, though, did not begin well. The delegation warned that the Persians would soon be on the way with the aim of conquering all the Greeks and that included those who lived in Sicily. Syracuse, they reminded him, was a great power and should join in the resistance. Should the Persians prevail in the Greek homeland, then they would come against him. Gelon, in reply, angrily pointed out that they had brought him no help in his wars with the Carthaginians. Nevertheless he said he would bring forces to help by sea and land, but on one condition: he must have supreme command of the Greek war effort. As with a similar request of the Argives, it met with a refusal. The Spartans did not propose to give this up to anyone. Gelon now tried to compromise, saying he would be happy with the command of either the land or the sea. Here the Athenians in the delegation intervened. They declared they were willing to take orders from the Spartans, but no others. Should the Spartans relinquish command of the fleet then it must devolve to them. At this Gelon brought the interview to a close and bade the ambassadors farewell, remarking as he did so that it would appear they had many commanders but few troops.

In truth, it is unlikely Gelon would have anyway been in a position to offer any real aid due to his domestic difficulties. War between Greeks and Carthaginians in Sicily was not constant but was punctuated by intervals of peace and truce. Now one of these periods of calm was coming to an end, a large Carthaginian army was preparing to attack and Gelon had to be ready to meet it. The Greek world was being threatened simultaneously from East and West. This gave rise to a theory that the assault was co-ordinated. Xerxes had, as we know, many Phoenicians in his fleet and Carthage was a Phoenician foundation. So it was claimed the two powers acted in concert to crush their mutual opponent. Herodotus knows nothing of this and it seems to have originated with a later historian, Ephorus. In actuality it has little to recommend it and it looks like the concoction of a third rate academic wishing to establish a cheap reputation for cleverness.

Our concern is naturally with the Greeks of the homeland but it would not be right to leave Gelon without recording his subsequent fate. In the next year he beat off the Carthaginians and overwhelmed their forces in a great battle at Himera. He did not, either, forget the warning that the Persians might come against Sicily should they conquer Greece. In order to shore up his position, he sent a man to Delphi with a large sum of money. Should the Persians prevail, he was to turn this over to them with the usual tokens of earth and water. If the Greeks won he was simply to return home.[11]

On their way back from Syracuse, the Greek delegates put in at Corcyra where they appealed, as they had to Gelon. Here the initial response seemed to be more promising, for the Corcyreans said that they would join in the common cause. In the event, they proved to be equivocators. When the war began, their fleet put to sea but went no further than the Peloponnese. The Corcyreans, like the ruler of Syracuse, had decided to wait and see who was going to win. Later, when the victorious Greeks began to scrutinize their behaviour, they claimed they had been prevented from going any further by adverse winds.[12]

When it came to the turn of the Cretans to be asked, an oracle, as with Argos, was invoked. Delphi recalled some mythological disasters the island had allegedly once suffered and advised the Cretans to keep out of this war. They complied.[13]

As our narrative in the next three chapters will demonstrate, the unity of those Greek states who had determined on resistance was to be a fragile thing, and was at times threatened greatly by internal quarrels and disagreements which will be treated in detail. It will not be out of place, at this point, to attempt a broad classification of those who medized or took the Persian side in order the better to understand their often differing motives, and the role they were to play in the events of the next two years. These people fall into three broad categories.

As we saw, the Greeks who met at the Isthmus in 481 BC recognized that many states were blameless. Lying in the path of the Persian advance, they had the choice of submission or destruction. Long before Xerxes' invasion, we saw that Macedon, faced with this choice, had elected to yield. In 480 BC, as we shall see, the Thessalians decided to take the same course but the Phocians opted for resistance and were to pay for it.

The equivocators we have also met with. Gelon and his like had no desire to have a Persian master. So long as Xerxes was at a distance, they saw no reason why they should yield to him. Once he drew near this would change and preparations were made to meet with this eventuality.

Those who opted for voluntary medism did so for a number of different reasons. We may recall that Argos, in part at least, acted from hatred and fear of their long time rivals, Sparta. Earlier we saw how, in the time of Darius, two Phocaean brothers had called him in because they wished to get the better of domestic rivals. Factionalism is to be observed in many of the medising states. As we shall see, Thebes was then, and still now, regarded as the chief medizer in this war, but yet there was a faction there, too, which opposed this policy.[14]

The decision to medize or not acquired a certain urgency as 481 BC progressed. Sometime in the spring of that year, Xerxes quitted Susa to begin the campaign. As he did so there occurred an eclipse of the sun. Natural phenomena of this type were taken very seriously indeed by peoples of that time, for they were held to be a message from the gods. Elucidation of meaning was called for, so Xerxes sent for the Magi. These men formed a kind of priestly caste among the Persians and were held to be skilled in the arts of divination. They now told Xerxes that the sun represented the Greeks, while the moon represented the Persians, so it was clear who was going to emerge victorious from this particular war. Thus reassured, Xerxes went on his way until he came to a place called Critalla, in Cappadocia, where the army was mustering. From there he led it through Phrygia. Crossing the Halys, he came to Lydia and passed the winter of that year in Sardis.[15]

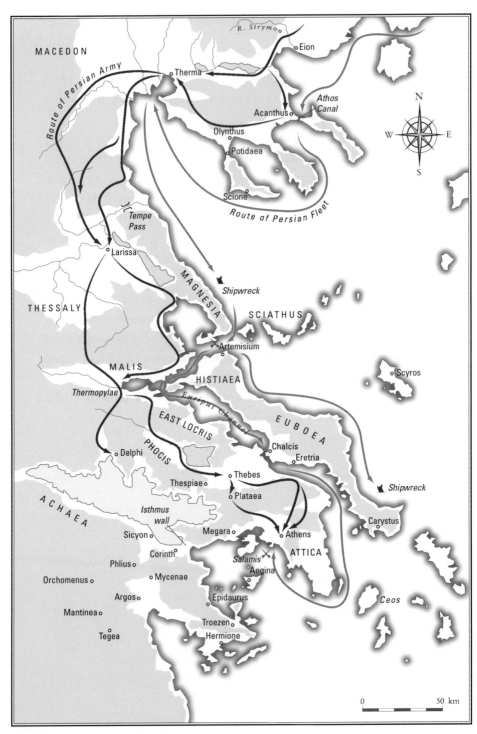

Map 3: Xerxes' invasion route, 480 BC.

Chapter 5

Thermopylae and Artemisium (480 BC)

With the coming of spring in 480 BC, Xerxes and his unwieldy army set out from Sardis once more. He paused briefly at the site of Troy to pay his respects and then at last came to Abydus, where the bridges over the Hellespont were ready. At this point, too, he was joined by his navy. The king then mounted a throne from which he could see both army and fleet spread out below him. At first he rejoiced but then started to cry as he reflected that in a hundred years' time not a man of them would be alive. Artabanus who happened to be to hand observed that life was indeed sad and brought with it so many troubles that death could seem like a release. The conversation then turned to the business in hand and Artabanus warned of two great enemies, the sea and the land. Should there be a storm then on the sea there would not be a harbour large enough to take the fleet. As for the land, the farther one went into such a poor country, the greater the danger of starvation as supplies ran low. Xerxes replied that a man had to take risks and that his ancestors would have accomplished nothing if they had not done so. The desire to win military glory was plainly strong with him. Artabanus then said he should keep a close eye on the Ionians in his fleet as they could be potential traitors. Xerxes, however, dismissed the notion. As things turned out, Artabanus was wrong about the Ionians but right about the dangers of land and sea but, even at a distance of over two thousand years, we can sense how he might be an irritant with his constant lecturing. Xerxes seems to have thought so because he now sent him back home but not in disgrace, for he appointed him steward of the royal house in his absence.

On the day appointed to begin the crossing of the Hellespont, Xerxes prayed to the rising sun and made offerings to the waters. It is said to have taken seven days and nights for the host to cross to Sestus on the opposite side in Thrace. Here the gods gave a sign: a mare gave birth to a hare. Nobody seems to have interpreted it correctly then but those who were wise after the event said it meant Xerxes would go to Greece in splendour but run out of it for his life.

From Sestus, the land army made its way to Derisius. It was accompanied by the fleet which first waited a little at Cape Sarpedon but then came to Derisius, too, where it was beached as the army rested in the plain nearby. Setting out from here, again, the army continued its advance but now in three columns. One took the road by the coast, next marched that commanded by Xerxes in person and finally there was a third further inland. A bridge was ready for the crossing of the River Strymon. The crossing place was known as Nine Ways. Crossroads are traditionally places where the upper world meets the underworld and it is this which seems to have led the Persians to sacrifice, by burial, nine boys and nine girls.

The rough terrain in places slowed progress but the natives proved to be no problem as they had, it will be remembered, been subdued by Darius' generals. At one stage, lions did prove to be a hazard, as they attacked the baggage train in search of camel meat. When the Chalcidic peninsula was reached, Xerxes made a detour to Acanthus, whose people had worked on the Mount Athos canal and to whom he now gave a gift. His fleet he ordered to pass through the canal and make for Therma in Macedon. Here they joined up once more with the army which had marched across the northern part of the peninsula.[1]

As we might have expected, the Greeks had not been inactive either. Early in 480 BC, while Xerxes was still at Abydus, the delegates of the league convened once more at the Isthmus. There they received ambassadors from Thessaly. These asked that a force be sent to the pass of Tempe between Thessaly and Macedonia to block Xerxes' advance. They could not be expected to defend it on their own and if help were not coming then they would medize.

The situation in Thessaly was a complex one. Power rested with a number of great baronial families and in 485 BC one of these, the Aleudae, had invited Xerxes to come to Greece. Their aim, as we have seen in other cases, was to get the upper hand over the other families. These had no enthusiasm for medizing, but they agreed to send the tokens of earth and water. Their motive resembled somewhat that of Gelon. He had been ready to submit if the Persians came near, and that day had already dawned for the Thessalians since the Persians had received the surrender of Macedon and were dangerously close. The gesture of 485 BC had two consequences. In the first place, it did not in fact allow the Aleudae to achieve the mastery they sought, while the rest had bought some security with an insincere submission. Now there was to be a change. The Persians were coming. For the Aleudae this would mean the domination they wanted. For the rest there was a dilemma. Would they now yield in reality or would they repudiate their allegiance?

Their answer was a qualified yes. Those who came to the Isthmus represented a party that would fight the Persians, provided they had help from their fellow-Greeks. Those Greeks decided that forces should indeed be sent to Tempe, and there is reason to believe Themistocles' influence had been decisive in setting this enterprise afoot and he himself commanded the Athenian contingent.

A force of hoplites was despatched by boat through the Euripus channel. When it reached Achaea it proceeded on foot to Tempe. Stiffened by a cohort of Thessalian cavalry, this army prepared to block this pass which led from Macedon to Thessaly. But they did not long stay there. Alexander of Macedon who, as we know, had medized, approached them. Now and later, we shall see him trying to gain the favour of both sides in order to stand well with whoever should win. At this point he told his audience of the size of the

Persian army and warned they would be overwhelmed. The desire to be of service to the Greeks is plain enough but there is a suspicion Alexander was also thinking of something else, something closer to home. Should the Persian army be blocked, even for a little while, it would devour his and his subjects' substance. Thus he would wish to have them out of his lands as soon as possible. His arguments were reinforced by a discovery the Greeks had made for themselves: there were other ways into Thessaly and their position could thus be turned. There was nothing for it but to abandon Tempe and return home. The Thessalians, for their part, being now deprived of support, took the Persian part.[2]

With Thessaly lost, the allies at the Isthmus had to find a new line of defence and decided on Thermopylae, a pass narrower than that of Tempe. At the same time the Persian navy had to be confronted so the fleet was also despatched and took up position at Artemisium.

Artemisium lies on the northern tip of Euboea and the intention seems to have been that the fleet should command the strait between the island of Sciathus and the mainland. The land forces were nearby and they were to keep in touch with the navy so that both might act in concert. Thermopylae actually lay on a narrow coastal road which was bordered on one side by the Malic gulf and the other by the mountain range of Oeta, of which the highest peak was Callidromus. Today, silting has rendered the place considerably broader. Then at its western end (dubbed the 'Western Gate' by the historian G.B. Grundy) by the River Phoenix, which flowed into the Aesopus, it was no broader than the width of a carriage. The same was true at the 'Eastern Gate' (again the name was given by Grundy), which lay near a village called Alpeni. In the middle there were hot springs from which the place derives its name (Thermopylae or 'Hot Gates') and here the pass broadened to some fifty feet. Behind this 'Middle Gate' there was, at this time, the remains of an old wall which had been built by the Phocians to keep out their enemies, the Thessalians.[3]

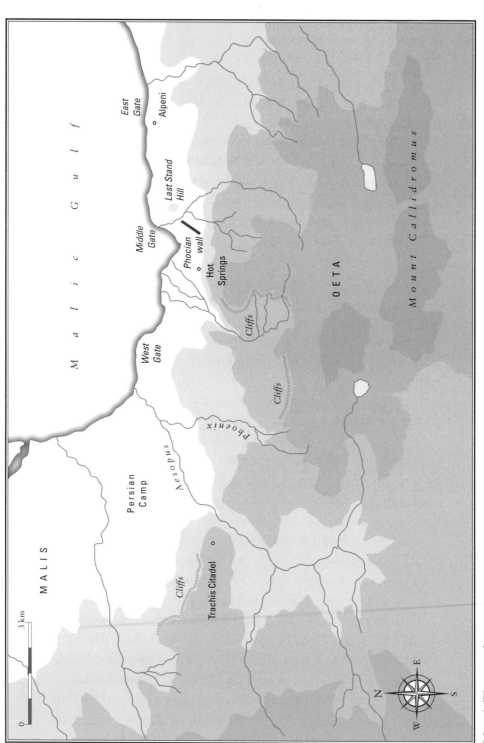

Map 4: Thermopylae.

The army, which was now to attempt to block Xerxes' advance, was commanded by the Spartan king Leonidas. In view of the patina of legend which Thermopylae has acquired – to which we will return in due course – it is important to realize he did not just lead Spartans. His force was said to number some 7,000 and not only were there contributions from the rest of the Peloponnese, but Thespiae and Thebes sent men from Boeotia, as did the Locrians and the Phocians. The presence of the Thebans requires comment and elucidation. That Thebes was preparing to medize seems by now to have been common knowledge, but Leonidas decided to put the matter to the test and summoned troops from there. In fact, Thebes, as so often happened in Greek states, was split into factions between pro- and anti-Persian. Those who now came to Leonidas were almost certainly members of the anti-Persian party. They would naturally wish to fight for the Greek cause while their opponents would only be too happy to be rid of people who might make nuisances of themselves when the time came to openly declare for Xerxes.

From among the Spartans, Leonidas recruited only men who had sons living, but this prudent move should not be taken to mean he and his men were embarking on a suicide mission. The expedition was hazardous but the expectation seems to have been that Leonidas and his men would hold out for some time and certainly long enough for reinforcements to arrive. The attitude of the allies can be gauged from the fact that the Spartans did not send more troops because they were celebrating one of their festivals, the Carneia, and the rest of Greece was busy with the Olympic Games.[4]

When he came to Thermopylae, Leonidas took up his position at the Middle Gate. Here he soon made an unpleasant discovery. There was a path over the Callidromus by which his position could be turned. To guard this, he sent the Phocians up the mountain.[5]

We left Xerxes at Therma. He lingered there a little, taking time out to do some sightseeing at the gorge of Tempe. As a good Zoroastrian, he showed due appreciation of its natural beauties. His route from Therma into Thessaly is still a matter of dispute among experts and all that can be usefully said is that he most likely continued with his advance in three columns. Thessaly, as we know, was now his and Xerxes only stopped there for a day to hold races between Persian and Thessalian horses, which the Persians won. The three pronged advance pushed on with one column marching by way of the gulf of Pagae. In this way the Persian army came at last to the level ground about Trachis, which lay a little way before the Western Gate to Thermopylae.[6]

Seeing the size of the Persian army, some of the Greeks were for retreating but the Locrians and Phocians demanded they stay. Leonidas consented but sent out messengers with an urgent appeal for reinforcements.

Xerxes, meantime, had sent forward a horseman to see what the Greeks were doing. He was puzzled to see some of the Spartans before the Phocian wall indulging in exercise or combing their hair, and when he reported this back to Xerxes, the king shared that puzzlement and decided to seek expert advice. He therefore sent for the exiled Spartan king Demaratus, who was travelling in his entourage. We have met this man before when we saw him credited wrongly with aiding Xerxes get the throne. Here we see his true position and standing at the Persian court. He was kept about the place to give the king information on things Greek, when he was asked for it, and while he was allowed to express opinions, Xerxes was in no way bound to share them.

Once before on this expedition, Xerxes had made enquiries of him. As he was curious to know more about the people he was marching against, he, while his army was assembling at Sestus, asked Demaratus to satisfy his curiosity. Life at court had taught the Spartan to be wary of Xerxes' moods, so he asked if he wanted to hear something pleasant or the truth. Xerxes told him to speak freely. Demaratus then told him the Spartans were the best warriors in Greece. They would not yield even if everybody else did and, irrespective of the number of their opponents, they would fight him. Xerxes in reply wondered how the Spartans would indeed fight against such odds, particularly as they had no one single commander but were free to follow their own inclinations. Demaratus said he, and his fellow Spartans, would not seek to engage in unequal combat but, if it were forced upon them, they would. Free men they were, but they obeyed Sparta's laws and these laws required them never to retreat but to die in battle. That conversation ended at this point with an incredulous Xerxes good humouredly dismissing Demaratus. Now, again, Xerxes asked what was happening. Demaratus told him the Spartans at the pass had come to fight and that it was their custom to comb their hair before a great ordeal. He added that, if Xerxes overcame these men and the other Spartans still at home, then the world would be his. Xerxes, however, was still unconvinced of the quality of those who faced him.

For four days the Persian made no move. It may very well be Xerxes was expecting the Spartans to retreat but there will have been another consideration which also weighed with him. We know that it was intended both army and fleet should act in concert and, in the present instance, ships would be able to outflank the Greek position. The fleet had not yet appeared, as it had experienced certain difficulties on the way, which will be treated in detail at the appropriate point in our narrative.

Suffice to say that, when it had not arrived on the fifth day, Xerxes became impatient and went over to the attack. He sent Medes and Cissians (one of the subject peoples) against the Spartans. These came on in waves but were hampered by the narrow space and by the fact that their spears were shorter than those of the Spartans. These suffered losses but they were much lighter than those they inflicted. A notable feature of their fighting style was to pretend to retreat, but in good order. Then they would suddenly wheel round on their pursuers to inflict great casualties on them. Xerxes eventually pulled out the Medes and Cissians and sent the elite Immortals in their place, but they could make no headway either and so ended the first day's fighting. On the next, the Persians were no more successful as the Greeks conserved their strength by taking turns to stand by nation in line. Again Xerxes was obliged to call off his attack.

At this point the solution to the king's obvious dilemma presented itself in the person of a man called Ephialtes. He told him of the path over the mountain, by which Leonidas could be taken in the rear and offered to guide a force along it. Xerxes accepted with alacrity and, in Herodotus' vivid phrase, 'about lamp lighting time' the detachment set out under the command of one Hydarnes. Its progress is a tribute to Persian skill in mountain warfare, for it seems to have marched without lights through the night. Just as dawn was breaking, the Persians came to the height guarded by the Phocians. The first these learned of what was happening was when the dead leaves rustled under the feet of the enemy. They sprang to arms, but under a volley of arrows retreated further up the mountain. The Persians, who had other quarry in mind, simply ignored them and began the downwards descent.

It is said that Leonidas first learned something was amiss when his resident seer, Megistias, inspected the entrails at the morning sacrifice and assured his audience that they wore a grim aspect. Be that as it may, news of events was also brought by some Greek deserters from the Persian side and by Phocians who had made it down the mountain side: in a few hours Hydarnes and his men would be behind them.

Leonidas called a council of war and announced that he and his Spartans did not propose to desert the post to which they had been assigned. As Demaratus had predicted to Xerxes, they would obey their laws. The other contingents were under no such obligation and so he dismissed them, for they might prove useful in the other battles to come. Besides the Spartans, there remained with him the Thespians and the Thebans. It is said he kept the latter as hostages for their city's good behaviour, but this is not likely. Somebody facing what Leonidas was about to face would not keep the unwilling around him. Rather the Thebans must have remained voluntarily, as did the Thespians. Their desire to fight on had not diminished and anyway they had nowhere to go. They were, in effect, exiles from Thebes. The medizers were now in control there and would not receive them.

Xerxes now poured a libation to the rising sun and then set his forces in motion once more. On this, the last day of Thermopylae, the Greeks determined to take as many of the enemy with them as possible. So they advanced into the broader area before the Phocian wall. The Persians were driven on with whips by their officers to be met with the spears of the Spartans and, when these broke, swords. Others who did not perish in this way were trampled underfoot or fell into the sea. Leonidas himself was killed and, after a great struggle, his body was rescued by his men.

Then came the news that Hydarnes' men were approaching. The remaining Greeks pulled back behind the wall to make their last stand on a small hillock. The Thebans at this point decided they had had enough and rushed to the enemy to surrender. Xerxes granted them their lives but the remaining Greeks held out to the last with swords, or even hands and teeth, until they were surrounded by the Persians and perished under a hail of missiles.[7]

After the battle Xerxes, according to one report, had another conversation with Demaratus. After admitting the Spartan had been right all along he asked how many more of them there were and how they might best be overcome. Demaratus said there were about 8,000 of the Spartans, and the best way to deal with them was to seize the island of Cythera at the base of the Peloponnese. From here a campaign could be mounted against the Spartans and, while they were kept in play, the king could deal with the rest of Greece, and Sparta would then be isolated.

As Demaratus pointed out this would involve detaching part of the fleet. Achaemenes, who was a brother of the king and commander of the fleet, objected. He accused Demaratus of being envious of Xerxes' good fortune and of being a potential traitor. He urged keeping the fleet intact, saying the enemy would never attack such numbers and that the original plan of combined operations should still be adhered to. Xerxes said he would take his brother's advice but that he was satisfied that Demaratus spoke honestly. He reminded those present that Demaratus was their guest and must not be slandered.

There are certain suspicions to be entertained about this anecdote, since it may attribute too much influence to a man of Demaratus' lowly position. It has to be admitted, though, that the generosity or, at least, magnanimity Xerxes showed towards Demaratus is partly reflected in his treatment of the Thebans. As we saw, he spared their lives but, since the Persians prized courage above all other virtues, he had them branded on the forehead as cowards. With Leonidas, his chivalric instincts deserted him and he besmirched his own reputation. So far from acknowledging his opponent's great courage, Xerxes desecrated his body. He had Leonidas' head cut off and stuck on a pole. The losses he had received may have had something to do with bringing out this worst side of Xerxes' character. He would appear to have fears over their effect on morale. That, at least, is how we may interpret the detail that, when a little later he invited people from the fleet to view the battlefield, he had all but a thousand of the Persian corpses buried beforehand.[8]

Viewing the matter dispassionately, it must be stated flatly that there is no doubt Thermopylae was a military disaster for the Greeks. The Persian invasion had only been halted for a little, and the way into central Greece now lay open to them with consequences we narrate in our next chapter. Failure to guard the route over Mount Oeta was a major factor in that defeat and it may, in equal measure, be attributed to Phocian failure to do their duty and to Leonidas' excessive faith in their ability to do so. But blame must also be apportioned elsewhere. Whatever one makes of Leonidas' very Spartan decision to die rather than desert the post to which he had been assigned, we have to remember that failure on the part of the allies as a whole to send adequate reinforcements put him where he felt he had to make the sacrifice he did.

But we also have to recognize that this disaster was not viewed dispassionately then and has not often been so viewed since. The battle rapidly became the subject of legend and a paradigm of doomed heroism. Paladins fought here who were to be seen as beyond criticism. Tales were soon told of these heroes. An oracle, which is most likely to have been composed later, proclaimed that Sparta herself would be destroyed unless a king sacrificed his life for her. Leonidas himself is said to have demonstrated his coolness and courage on the morning of the last day, when he told his men to take breakfast quickly as they would have supper in Hades. The king, who said this, found a worthy follower in a certain Dieneces. When he was told the Persian arrows were so thick that they would blot out the sun, he said this was all to the good as it meant they would be able to fight in the shade. Conversely anybody who, for whatever reason, fell short of the ideal was execrated. Two soldiers, Eurytus and Aristodemus, had been sent back to Alpeni village because of eye troubles. When they heard that the final battle was about to begin, Eurytus had his helot lead him there, while Aristodemus elected to remain where he was. A variant has him taking a message and dawdling on the way back. Another messenger, Pantites, who had gone to Thessaly, also survived. Both fell under a boycott when they got back to Sparta. Pantites committed suicide, but Aristodemus lived to perform feats of valour at Plataea.

Today monuments mark the battlefield and so it was also in antiquity. A stone lion in memory of Leonidas stood on the hillock where the last stand had taken place. On columns were epitaphs commemorating the seer Megistias, put up by his friend, the poet Simonides and all of those who fell, except the Spartans. They had a simple oft-quoted epitaph which said they lay there obedient to their country's laws. Thermopylae takes its place with such doomed enterprises as the Serbian Blackbird Fields or the Irish rebellion of 1916. Admired and held in awed reverence, it proved more inspirational than any victory.[9]

While it was being fought at Thermopylae, something had been happening too on the sea and it is to that we now have to turn.

When Xerxes left Therma it was clear that it would take him longer to reach Thermopylae than it would the fleet to reach the gulf of Pagasae, so he ordered it to wait for eleven days before following on. Ten of its fastest vessels headed straight for the island of Sciathus on a reconnaissance mission. There they fell in with three Greek ships who were keeping watch. The first from Troezen was captured and the captain was made a human sacrifice of. Herodotus vaguely hints at the possibility that his name Leon (Lion) was taken by them as some kind of omen. Another trireme from Aegina put up a great resistance and one marine in particular, Pytheas, distinguished himself. When the Persians took him prisoner, they dressed his wounds and then exhibited him to their comrades as a specimen of courage. The third Greek ship, an Athenian, was also taken but her crew managed to get ashore and make their way back to Athens by way of Thessaly. News of the encounter was flashed by fire signal from Sciathus to the main fleet at Artemisium. This seems to have caused some kind of panic and the fleet pulled back, possibly as far as Chalcis (although some scholars dispute this), but left lookouts on the heights of Euboea. Three of the Persian scouts ran ashore on a shoal between Magnesia and Sciathus. However, once this was marked, the main fleet followed and reached the coast of Magnesia. Herodotus says they lay between Casthania and Cape Sepias, but these places have not been identified exactly.[10]

As the Greeks were heading for Thermopylae and Artemisium, the people of Delphi asked the oracle what was to be done. It replied that they should pray to the winds. The Delphians spread the word about and it would seem the Athenians took it especially to heart, for now they prayed to Boreas, the north wind. Their prayers were answered for there now began one of those violent Aegean storms which, once experienced, are never forgotten. The Greeks, lying in the lee of Euboea, were safe but it was otherwise with the Persians. Where they had put in, there was not space or mooring for all the ships and only a few had been made fast; the rest lay off shore. When the first signs of the coming storm appeared some, quicker than others, managed to beach their ships. Many, however, were caught on the open sea and blown ashore and wrecked with great loss of life. The watchers on Euboea sent word of the disaster to the Greek fleet and thanksgiving was duly rendered to Poseidon, god of the sea. For three days, the storm raged and it was not until the fourth day that it blew itself out, enabling the Greeks to move once more and take up their former position at Artemisium.[11]

The Persians, for their part, had put to sea again and sailed along the coast to the bay of Pagasae. They now took up their position at Aphetae on the southern tip of Magnesia. A squadron of fifteen lagged behind the main body. These mistook the Greek ships for their own and made for them. As a result they were captured and their commanders interrogated. Now, when the Greeks could see the whole Persian fleet, they realized its losses had not been as great as they had hoped. Eurybiades, the Spartan in command, took fright at this and began to contemplate retreat. The Euboeans were greatly perturbed by the decision and asked Eurybiades to at least give them time to evacuate their families. When he refused, they came to Themistocles, who commanded the Athenian squadron, and asked him to intercede for them. They offered him a large bribe to do so. Themistocles offered some of this money to Eurybiades. The venal Spartan accepted and resolved the fleet should stay where it was. Themistocles dealt in a similar fashion with a Corinthian commander, Adeimantus, who was still proving difficult. When he still continued to talk of retreat, Themistocles bribed him as well. In due course we shall comment on the – to us – dubious morality of this and other monetary transactions of the national hero. For the moment, we shall merely observe how clever Themistocles showed himself to be. He calculated to a nicety just how much he needed to give Eurybiades and Adeimantus in order to achieve results and was, in consequence, able to keep some of the Euboeans' money for himself. Another tale of yet more bribery is worth recounting, even though it does not rest on such good authority. In this Architeles, captain of the Athenian state galley, threatened to sail away as he had not money to pay his crew. Themistocles worked upon the minds of the men so that they rushed Architeles and stole his dinner. Themistocles sent him some food, beneath which silver was concealed, and bade him eat up and use the money to pay his crew, otherwise he would have him charged with taking a bribe from the enemy.[12]

At Aphetae, the Persians continued to be busy. They counted their losses and made repairs. Nor had they lost sight of their objective of destroying the enemy. They despatched a squadron round Sciathus. This was then to sail down the coast of Euboea and turn into the Euripus channel. In this way they would come up behind the Greek fleet which would then be hemmed in on both sides by the two divisions of the Persians. Here another athlete plays an important part in Greek history. We already met Pheidippides the runner and his mission to Sparta, at the time of Marathon. Now he has a counterpart in Scyllias, a champion swimmer. This man was in the Persian fleet and had saved much property for them in the recent storm, although – and this reminds us of Themistocles – he had kept some for himself. Scyllias resolved to desert and is said to have swum across to Artemisium, keeping under water the whole time. Given the distance involved – some ten miles – we need not believe this and may safely assume he came by boat. At any rate, he now told the Greeks what was going on among the Persians and of the number of their losses.

The high command discussed what the deserter had to say and resolved to send out a detachment to deal with the Persians who were sailing down the coast of Euboea. In the event this decision does not seem to have been implemented immediately and, actually, in the course of events became otiose. What the Greeks did do almost at once was to take advantage of the diminished number of ships at Aphetae to make a trial of the naval capacity of the enemy.

They waited until the afternoon of the following day before coming out to attack. Here again we may recall Marathon since now, as then, the Persians were amazed at Greek audacity in view of the smallness of their numbers and the superior quality of their own ships. They therefore had no hesitation in sailing out to meet the foe. An extra incentive to action was to be found in Xerxes' promise of a reward for the first Greek vessel captured. The intent was to use superior numbers to encircle the Greeks. They, for their part, were ready with countermeasures. At a given signal, they fanned out in a circle with prows facing outward and sterns to the middle. Then, at a second signal, they attacked going prow to prow with their opponents. Thirty Persian ships were captured before night put a stop to the battle and both forces withdrew to their separate anchorages.

During the night, nature intervened yet again to the advantage of the Greeks, when another storm came on. This time it was not the winds but a great thunderstorm which brought with it torrents of rain, which caused flash floods and terrified the Persians at Aphetae. More important, this storm was responsible for destroying the fleet sent around to take the Greeks in the rear. It was driven ashore and wrecked on the rocks at a place called the Hollows of Euboea. Encouraged by news of this and by a stiffening of some more ships from Athens, the Greeks made another afternoon swoop. Most of the Persians seem to have been too demoralized to put to sea but the Greeks attacked and destroyed some Cilician ships, before retiring once more for the night.[13]

On the next day, the Persians went on the offensive. A variety of motives appear to have impelled them. As proud warriors, they could ill brook the defeats they had just suffered. They also feared what Xerxes, with his uncertain temper, might do to them if they did not improve their performance. The previous two days fighting had coincided with the first two days of the Battle of Thermopylae and the king seems to have sent a message across, calling on the fleet to come and help break the stalemate. About midday the Persian fleet sailed out to attack the waiting Greeks in a crescent formation. Very few details of the actual battle are on record but we do know the Persian ships fouled each other as they advanced on the Greeks, who were sailing in a half-moon formation. On their side, the Egyptians particularly distinguished themselves. Losses on both sides were heavy, with the Athenians suffering considerable damage. At evening, both sides drew apart and the Greeks were left in possession of the dead and the wrecks. The verdict was that the battle had resulted in stalemate, but the Greeks decided on withdrawal.

They had kept an observer at Trachis and this man now arrived in a galley with the news that the Persians had forced the pass of Thermopylae, and that Leonidas and his men were dead. Careful preparations were made for an orderly retreat. Fires were lit on the beach, at Themistocles' suggestion, to give the Persians the impression the Greeks did not propose to budge from their position. The Euboeans, it will be remembered, had asked for a delay so that they might evacuate their families and possessions. They had by this time got their herds together but, once more at Themistocles' advising, the sailors proceeded to slaughter and eat them.

The retreat down the Euripus channel now began with the Corinthians leading and the Athenians bringing up the rear. In all of the fighting, only one Greek ship had deserted the Persian side, even though the Ionians were said to be concerned at the fate of their fellow countrymen. On the beach at Artemisium, Themistocles declared he had a plan to detach more of them from the king's side. This he now carried out. As he made his way down the coast, he left scratched on the rocks, at places where water was to be found, messages urging the Ionians to defect. His reasoning was simple. If, as actually happened, the Ionians did not fall away from their allegiance, he might yet sow suspicions of them in Xerxes' mind when the king got to hear of it.[14]

Chapter 6

Salamis (480 BC)

With Thermopylae stormed the Persian advance by land continued. Two columns seem to be in question. One went along the coast through Locris, which had medized, reverted to the Greek side and now medized again. The second crossed by the hill routes into Doris, where no harm was done as the people here, too, were medizers. In any case, the Thessalians used their influence with Xerxes to see they were spared. They exercised this influence in exactly the opposite way when the army reached Phocis. Thessalians had long been traditional enemies of the Phocians and had, in a recent war, been worsted at their hands. They told the Phocians that they could persuade Xerxes to spare them, if they paid a sum of fifty talents. Just as Argos had taken the Persian side out of hatred for Sparta, so it was claimed Phocis had chosen the Greek side out of enmity to the Thessalians. Now they told the Thessalians they did not propose to play the traitor's part and refused to pay up. In consequence, the Persians, egged on by the Thessalians, ravaged the country, destroying everything in their path. Most of the Phocians got away, taking refuge in the mountains or among the Locrians. Some few were caught however and some women were raped so often that they died.

One column now headed in the direction of Delphi. It was believed Xerxes had sent them to plunder the shrine. This threw the inhabitants into a panic but word came from the god that he could look after his own. Most of the citizens nevertheless evacuated. As the Persians approached, a miracle occurred. Sacred weapons from the shrine were found lying outside, although no human hand had touched them. When the enemy came even closer, thunderbolts came from the sky and great rocks fell on them. The Persians fled in panic, pursued by the Delphians who were aided by two hoplites of superhuman size. We need not, I think, believe anything of this happened. Rather what we are looking at is a concoction by the priests of Delphi themselves. The Persians had ever shown Apollo a tender regard and held his oracles in esteem and those oracles, in turn, had consistently given prophecies favourable to them. Hence, we may beg leave to doubt if Xerxes turned on Delphi now but, once the war was over and the Greeks had won, some explanation had to be given for Delphi's deliverance and also for the stance it had so consistently taken. This looks like the best the priests of Delphi could come up with. To us it seems a trifle implausible but it appears to have worked. In an age of piety, nobody questioned it.

At the same time as this was allegedly going on, the other division of the army with Xerxes at its head had passed into Boeotia. This was a pro-Persian land from which the tokens of earth and water had come and was where the chief medizer Thebes was situated. Nevertheless Alexander of Macedon played a part akin to that of the Thessalians a little earlier, plainly with the intention of garnering as much goodwill as he could with both Greeks and Persians. In an otiose gesture, he sent around agents to the various towns to assure Xerxes' men that these places were indeed loyal. Two towns did not surrender and were visited with Xerxes' anger and burned to the ground. It had not been forgotten that Thespiae had sent men to Thermopylae and that they had remained there to the last with Leonidas and his Spartans. But although their town was destroyed, the inhabitants got away to the Peloponnese. The Plataeans had fought at Artemisium and, when the retreating Greek fleet got as far as Chalcis, they went ashore and managed to evacuate their fellow townsmen in time. Xerxes, we know, had reason enough to act as he did but some professed to believe that he had been put up to this by the Thebans.[1]

From Boeotia, Xerxes came to neighbouring Attica and so to Athens itself. He found himself in a deserted city, save for the

Acropolis. There a group of the citizens had barricaded themselves behind a wooden barrier on the Acropolis. The background to this circumstance must now be set forth.

Oracles have played a part in our narrative. We saw how, after the event, one had circulated to the effect that a king must die to save Sparta. Another which concerned the Euboeans may also date from a later period. They were warned that, when the Hellespont was bridged, they had best start moving their property. They were said, however, to have ignored this and so they found themselves still evacuating their flocks after the Battle of Artemisium.[2] We also saw – and these are more likely to be contemporary – two which advised the Greeks to call upon the winds for assistance. This brings us to arguably the most famous pair of all and they involved the Athenians.

With the threat from Xerxes becoming clear, they decided to approach the Delphic oracle to receive some hint of the future and possible advice on what might be done. Scholars argue as to whether this consultation took place in 481 or 480 BC. The earlier date is the more likely. In that year the Greeks had gathered at the Isthmus to see what might be done by human means to halt Xerxes. This would therefore be the most natural time to try and learn the divine will, rather than waiting until the next year when he was already on the march and about to enter Greece.

When the Athenian delegates entered the temple of Delphi, the prophecy of the oracle was of the gloomiest. They were told they should flee. The Persians were coming to bring destruction not only to their city but to others in Greece. Fire would consume their temples and blood would flow. Needless to say, the Athenian enquirers were somewhat shaken by this but, on the advice of a Delphian, approached the shrine as suppliants. This time the reply was slightly more hopeful but, as befitted an oracle, somewhat enigmatic. Attica would fall but a wooden wall would hold. The Athenians must still flee but they would encounter the enemy at Salamis where many men would perish.

The discouraging tone of the first response is not difficult to account for and points towards its authenticity. The problem with the second is the mention of Salamis. As a great battle did in fact take place there, we are still either looking at yet another concoction after the event or we are witnessing a remarkable instance of prescience. Certainty is impossible but, as we shall see in a moment, since the rest of the oracle would appear to be genuine, we might attribute the mention of Salamis to a reasoned deduction, or even a superhuman insight, by Delphi. If the Greeks were beaten out of the north, then the Persians would come that way and Salamis would prove to be of the greatest strategic importance. As we will now see, once the reference to the wooden wall was correctly interpreted, then there is a certain logic – and more than a logic – to the mention of Salamis.[3]

When word of what the oracle had said was brought to Athens, there was debate. Some, with the backing of professional seers who claimed to be able to interpret such things, said that the utterance must be taken literally and a wooden wall was to be built. Others said it was metaphorical and that ships were meant. Foremost among these was Themistocles. Some years before, he had foreseen the necessity to create a navy and recognized that the time had come to deploy it. To strengthen his case he pointed out that the oracle had spoken of 'divine' Salamis and not 'hateful' Salamis, which indicated a favourable outcome for them in any action fought there. Themistocles and his allies prevailed and it was resolved that, when the time came, the city would be evacuated by sea.[4]

Some of our information on these wars comes from writers active centuries after the event. Even the closest in time, Herodotus, was writing in the next generation. It is therefore good to have, at first sight anyway, something which seems, though later itself, to preserve the words of a decree passed then. The Athenians were in the habit of preserving on stone the decisions of their assemblies. In AD 1959, one such stone was discovered on which was engraved what is usually styled 'the Troezen decree'. This makes provisions for the evacuation of Attica, should the Persians arrive there. Stated briefly, the contents are as follows: non-combatants are to go to Troezen in the Peloponnese or Salamis island, a group is to remain on the Acropolis, elaborate details are given for manning the fleet and then despatching it to Artemisium and Salamis. Finally, all political exiles are required to return to Attica.

On the face of it, this is a most valuable document, but there are difficulties and doubts as to its real worth. In the form we have it, the decree dates from the third century BC, but we happen to know that there was knowledge of it in the fourth. So we have to ask ourselves if we really have here the exact words of a decree passed in the fifth century or could there have been later interpolations in the rewriting? There are those who would go even further and dismiss the whole thing as a forgery. If people could invent oracles after the event, then it is not beyond the bounds of possibility that somebody with a good grasp of history could have composed this later. The arguments are technical but suffice to say that there is, as yet, no agreement among experts on these points.[5]

On that last clause, the recall of the exiles, we do have further (and reliable) information. Exiles tended to gravitate naturally to the enemy side and throw in their lot with the Persians. The Pisistratids, it will be recalled, had pestered both Darius and Xerxes to restore them to power. In our last chapter we encountered Demaratus, refugee from Sparta, acting as adviser to Xerxes. It is true that the latter is shown to have had some kind of remorse, but little faith can be placed in the account which has come down to us. Demaratus is alleged to have tipped off the Spartans about Xerxes' invasion in the following way. As the roads in Persia were closely guarded, he scraped the wax from a pair of tablets and concealed a warning message beneath. The messenger carried these safely along the road and brought them to Sparta. The Spartans had the reputation of being somewhat slow-witted and did not know what to make of this offering until Gorgo, that precocious child now grown up and married to Leonidas, showed herself to be as percipient as ever. She scraped off the wax and read the message beneath. We may beg leave to doubt if any of this happened. For one thing, the size of the Persian preparations would have made clear to everyone what they were about, without need of a message from Demaratus. For another, we might well wonder why guards might not have their suspicions aroused when they encountered a man travelling with a set of blank tablets. The conclusion must be that Demaratus, as he travelled with Xerxes, harboured hopes that he, like the Pisistratids, was to be restored to power in his homeland.

The Athenians were now guarding against people like this. They were also striving to bring an end to factionalism. Struggles for power too often led to one party or another calling on the Persians for aid in the Greek state. Internal quarrels had now to be set aside in the interest of unity in the face of the common enemy.

Those who were recalled now were not permanent exiles but had been subjected to the peculiarly Athenian device of ostracism. Under this system a vote of the people was held and a politician, judged obnoxious or too powerful, was exiled for a period of ten years but without any loss of property or of the income therefrom.

Most prominent among those who had been ostracized was a man called Aristides, who had acquired the name of the Just. As he was to play a significant role in what was now to happen, we must say a little more about him. Like Themistocles, he had fought at Marathon and distinguished himself then. He was even said to have played a part in having Miltiades' aggressive tactics adopted. Though the pair had fought together then, they became political enemies in the 480s BC. Aristides had earned his name of the Just because of his honesty, which sometimes seemed to veer off into rigidity and an unbending determination never to compromise. Thus it is hardly surprising that such a character would be an opponent of the altogether subtler and more adaptable Themistocles. Their respective characters and attitudes to each other were encapsulated in a report that Aristides had alleged that Themistocles had made off with public funds. Their quarrel at last reached the point where, about 482 BC, Themistocles was able to engineer Aristides' ostracism. An anecdote related about this illustrates well that the moral high ground is a slippery place and dangerous to him who would climb it.

The Athenians voted on those to be ostracized by scratching their names on a potsherd and the man whose name occurred the most often was duly exiled. On this occasion a functional illiterate approached Aristides and asked him to write the name Aristides on his potsherd. When Aristides asked why, the man replied that he did not know him personally but was fed up of hearing him called the Just. Aristides said nothing but simply wrote his name as requested. Such was the man who now returned to play his part in the defence of his native city.[6]

At the fall of Thermopylae the Athenians seem briefly to have assumed that the land army which had been assembled, albeit too late, to reinforce Leonidas, would now advance into Boeotia and confront Xerxes there. They were soon disappointed for the Peloponnesians showed no disposition to move beyond the Isthmus and began to build a wall to fortify it, further securing it by demolishing the Scironian Way which led there from south of Megara. There were those who were prepared to castigate them now and in the next year for adopting a policy which placed the safety of the Peloponnese before that of Greece as a whole but, in their defence, it can be pointed out that Boeotia is the largest plain in Greece and thus particularly suited for the Persians' strongest arm, cavalry.[7]

There was nothing for it but to carry out the decision to evacuate provisionally made the year before. The Greek fleet, in its retreat from Artemisium, had by now got as far as the bay of Salamis and, at the request of the Athenian contingent, put in there. Themistocles reminded the people once more of the true meaning of the oracle's 'wooden wall' and urged immediate embarkation.

He was aided by what some took to be a portent. The Athenians believed a great snake lived in a temple on the Acropolis and every month put out a honey-cake for it. Now this cake was untouched, so it was divined that Athena, patroness of the city, had abandoned it and that they must follow.

So, they took ship variously to Troezen, Aegina and Salamis. As Xerxes was not far off, there was need of haste. But haste can bring hurry and confusion and terror. We are told, for instance, that there was much wailing and lamenting as people scattered. More important, some old men were simply left behind because they were too infirm to make the journey. The plight of domestic animals and family pets attracted the particular attention of some of our sources. As their masters took ship, many came to them and howled. One dog which belonged to Xanthippus, like Aristides a man recalled from exile, swam after his ship and followed all the way to Salamis only to die on reaching land.

Pay for the crews of the ships was proving to be something of a problem. Themistocles is said to have solved this with his habitual cleverness. A breastplate affixed to the statue of Athena had gone missing and he made search for it in the baggage of those departing and unearthed monies which were confiscated and devoted to paying the crews.

Not all scholars of the present day believe this particular story. We may place more confidence in the report that the Areopagus, the ancient council of Athens whose powers were gradually being eroded by the new democracy, voted a sum of money for the upkeep of the fleet. This generosity must be seen in the light of something else which happened now. Cimon, son of Miltiades, led a group of young men to the Acropolis to dedicate the bridles of their horses to Athena. They then went to man the ships, for rowers not cavalry was what the situation called for. Both those who sat on the Areopagus and Cimon and his companions belonged to the richer classes and were not always friendly to democracy. Being of an oligarchic temperament, they would not be natural allies of the

Persian and Median warriors, Persepolis. (*Jenny Keaveney*)

The King fights a demon, Persepolis. (*Jenny Keaveney*)

Subjects bring tribute to the King, Persepolis. (*Jenny Keaveney*)

The King enthroned in majesty, Persepolis. (*Jenny Keaveney*)

A view of Persepolis today. (*Jenny Keaveney*)

The Marathon battlefield. (*Photo by kind permission of Christiane Casale*)

A modern statue of Miltiades at the
Marathon battlefield. (*Jenny Keaveney*)

Soros: the burial mound of the Athenian dead at Marathon. (*Jenny Keaveney*)

The Bay of Marathon. (*Jenny Keaveney*)

The Hill of Kolonos, the site of the Spartans' last stand. (*Jenny Keaveney*)

A view of the pass of Thermopylae from the Hill of Kolonos. (*Jenny Keaveney*)

A modern statue of Leonidas at the pass of Thermopylae. (*Jenny Keaveney*)

A view of the site of the Battle of Plataea from the Akropolis of Plataea. (*Jenny Keaveney*)

Mount Cithaeron. (*Jenny Keaveney*)

The Bay of Salamis, looking northward. (*Jenny Keaveney*)

Bust of Themistocles. (*Archivio Fotografico della Soprintendenza Speciale per i beni archeologici di Roma e Ostia*)

Olympias, a modern replica of a Greek trireme, arriving at Tolon. (*John Coates © The Trireme Trust*) mass of democrats who manned the fleet. In the next year (479 BC) before Plataea there was to be strain requiring the attention and skill of Aristides. But now both high and low were of one mind, as they made ready to fight the Persians.[8]

This then makes clear why Xerxes found Athens to be virtually deserted on his arrival there, except for those behind the wooden barrier on the Acropolis. Those there formed two groups. Some simply did not have the money to enable them to make for Salamis. We have just noted the shortage of public funds. What was available went to pay those who manned the fleet. There was no surplus available to aid the refugees. The second group comprised those who rejected Themistocles' interpretation of the oracle. They still believed an actual wooden wall was meant. Xerxes immediately set about dislodging them. The Persians took up position on the Areopagus, the hill opposite the Acropolis, and shot fire arrows into the wooden barricade. Still the defenders held out and rolled boulders down on their attackers. But, at last, the Persians showed yet again the same skill in mounting a seemingly impregnable place as they had at Sardis in the time of Croesus. A detachment made its way up by a precipitous way which had been left undefended. The Persians then swarmed over the Acropolis, slaughtering the inhabitants and burning and looting the temple. On the very next day, though, Xerxes' attitude changed. He ordered the Pisistratid exiles to go up to the Acropolis and sacrifice there in their usual manner. This is obviously something of a puzzle. Herodotus thought he might have had another bad dream or simply an uneasy conscience. It may very well be that we have here another example of Xerxes' erratic behaviour, but yet another explanation is possible. Now that Athens was in his hands and duly punished for the sacrilege at Sardis in the Ionian revolt, Xerxes simply intended to hand her over once more to the rule of the Pisistratids. At the moment of sacrifice it was reported that a sacred olive-tree, which had just been burned, now put out a new shoot. Of course, it could be claimed later that this meant democratic Athens would rise again but, at this time, it might very well have been interpreted to mean that Pisistratid rule would flourish once more.[9]

With the evacuation of Athens complete, the Athenian squadron rejoined the rest of the Greek fleet at Salamis. By now the Persian fleet was at Phaleron. At first the Persians had not believed that the Greek fleet had retreated from Artemisium, refusing to give credence to a man who came with the news from Histiaea. Convinced at last, they came first to Artemisium and then to Histiaea, which they overran together with its territory. At this point they took time out to inspect the bodies on the field of Thermopylae, as described in our last chapter. Then they waited another three days to allow the army to advance before heading down the Euripus channel. As their main objective was the Greek fleet, they largely ignored Euboea and its towns.[10]

The news of the fall of Athens caused consternation in the Greek fleet and some commanders prepared to flee. A semblance of order was restored and it was resolved that the fleet should fight at the Isthmus. During the night which followed, a man called Mnesiphilus came to Themistocles. He had been his tutor and he pointed to him the extreme impolity of such a move, since it would mean that the fleet would then break up and all would disperse to their own homes. Some scholars wonder if a man of Themistocles' intelligence really needed somebody else to tell him this, but it could also be argued that it is a tribute to Themistocles' wit that he could see the force of another's argument and make it his own. At any rate, he came privately to Eurybiades and presented Mnesiphilus' arguments to him, pretending he himself had thought of them. Eurybiades consented to reconvene the meeting.

Once they had come together, Themistocles, without waiting for Eurybiades to announce the purpose of the meeting, began a vigorous speech. He was interrupted by the Corinthian commander who observed that if you started to race before the signal you got whipped. Themistocles replied that if you started late you did not win it at all. He then proceeded to make his case.

He carefully made no reference to the danger of dispersal, should they budge from where they were. Instead he brought forward arguments of his own. If they went to the Isthmus they would fight in the open sea and, with their smaller numbers, would be at a definite disadvantage. Even if they won they would, by withdrawal, lose still more Greek territory. Moreover, where the Persian fleet would go, so would their army. By retreating to the Isthmus, all they would do would be to draw the Persians there. On the other hand, if they fought at Salamis, the narrows would be advantageous to their smaller fleet and a battle here would be in defence of the Peloponnese, just as much as one fought at the Isthmus and, in addition, much of the rest of Greece would be saved.

Affairs took a nastier turn when the Corinthian, in an effort to prevent matters being put to the vote, told Themistocles to be quiet as he was now a man without a city. Themistocles replied that, so long as the Athenians had their fleet, they had a city. He then told Eurybiades that, if they withdrew to the Isthmus, the feared dispersal would take place and the Athenians would lead it. We saw how the Ionians proposed to sail west at the time of their revolt. Now, Themistocles threatened the Athenians would make for Sicily where they already had interests and found a new city there. This threat seems to have been a deciding factor, for it was decided that the Greeks should stand and fight at Salamis.[11]

There had been a council of war on the Persian side as well. As might be expected, since it was presided over by an autocrat, there was greater unanimity. Guessing what their master wanted, all of the commanders, save one, advised giving battle. The dissenter was arguably the strangest of all those commanders, Artemisia from Halicarnassus, the hometown of Herodotus. As a subject she brought the contingent when summoned to the levy, but she was the only woman to do so. Curiously the macho men of Persia do not seem to have been troubled by her presence and even came to admire her, although their Athenian enemies felt resentment at having to fight a woman. Now she dared to counsel delay. Athens, his chief prize, was already his and it would be dangerous for Xerxes to take on the Greeks, as they were better sailors. Better to wait, as shortage of supplies would soon lead them to disperse. Artemisia's friends began to fear for her, while her enemies rejoiced, since both thought her plain speaking would provoke Xerxes. But they were mistaken. As with Demaratus, Xerxes valued an honest opinion, even though he now decided to press on with his plan of attack.

His first move seems to have been a feint by sea and land. Towards evening, a day or two before the battle proper, the fleet, or a portion of it, put out to sea in the direction of Salamis, only to return almost immediately to its base at Phaleron. This manoeuvre may have been carried out in conjunction with a quickly aborted march against the Peloponnese, if a rationalized explanation of yet another of Herodotus' miraculous stories is accepted. In this Demaratus and a man called Dicaeus were taking a walk in Attica when they saw a cloud of dust rising from Eleusis, together with voices singing. This they interpreted as supernatural and as boding ill to Xerxes and his army, but wisely decided to keep this interpretation to themselves. Moderns, as we have observed, have another explanation. The dust may have been caused by an army about to make a sortie against the Peloponnese.

Whatever the truth of this, Xerxes' feint had the effect of unsettling the Greeks and they began to squabble again. One party castigated Eurybiades for his decision to stay at Salamis, while another insisted he had been correct. Themistocles saw that, if it came to a vote, it might go against him, so he slipped out and summoned Sicinnus, who was his slave and tutor to his children. He despatched him to the Persians to tell them the Greeks were afraid and getting ready to flee. Further, they were riven with dissension and half of them would desert once the attack was mounted. Message delivered, Sicinnus got quickly away.

Of course what he had said was a piece of mendacity. Themistocles had set out to fool the King in order to bring about the clash he sought. Under assault from the Persians, the Greeks would have no choice but to fight and Xerxes fell for it. We know that Themistocles was a clever man and, as we saw from Darius' dealings with Histiaeus, for instance, there may have been some kind of perception that, speaking generally, Persians might not be as clever anyway as Greeks. But that is not really a consideration here. What is a consideration is that Xerxes had no reason to suppose Greeks would act in any other way. From Marathon to Artemisium they had shown themselves to be great fighters who could put up a strong resistance, but the Persians were familiar with another of their characteristics, a distinct tendency to fall out among themselves and betray each other. As early as Cyrus, this had manifested itself when Miletus chose to accept the terms it was offered although the other Ionian cities did not. Their behaviour subsequently will have led the king to expect treachery and dissension. When suitable pressure was applied as it had, for instance, been at Lade, there was, at the very least, a possibility some would cut and run. Hence there is no need to see this incident as fabulous. Both parties to the transaction acted exactly as we might expect them to. Xerxes had every reason to believe that the Greeks might flee and Themistocles exploited that belief.[12]

Responding to Themistocles' message, the Persians began to move under cover of night. On the western wing or Persian right were placed the Phoenicians, while the Ionians were to be found on the eastern or left wing. There is doubt about the order of the ships in between these two extremes, but in one account Cypriots were next to the Phoenicians and then followed from left to right by the Cilicians, Pamphylians and Lycians. The position of the Egyptians, as we shall soon see, is a matter of some dispute. Before setting out, however, the Persians placed a garrison on the island of Psyttaleia. The intent was to preserve friends and destroy enemies carried there.[13]

All the while the Persians were getting into position, the Greeks do not seem to have been aware of what was going on and continued with their squabbling. News of the situation was brought to them by Aristides. An earthquake had lately occurred and he had been despatched to Aegina to fetch cult objects which would placate the gods. Themistocles, after despatching his message to Xerxes, had rejoined the meeting. Aristides now called him out. Their longstanding rivalry was forgotten for the sake of the common good, as Aristides told him the debate had now become academic; the Greeks were surrounded. Delighted, Themistocles replied that he had engineered this. For the rest, he said that if he told the meeting what had happened, nobody would believe him, so he asked Aristides to give the commanders his news in person. But even now most of the commanders refused to believe Aristides and continued with the futile debate. Then came confirmation of what he had to say. A ship of Tenos deserted the Persian side and brought the same news. For this service the name of the Tenians was inscribed on the Serpent Column that commemorated the victory and whose remains are still to be seen in the Hippodrome in Istanbul.[14]

So, it was borne in at last upon the Greeks that they had no choice but to fight where they were. Just before the crews embarked, Themistocles addressed the Athenian contingent. He set before them the worst and the best in human nature and urged them to imitate the best. A stimulus of a different sort was applied on the Persian side. Xerxes had not been entirely happy with his fleet's performance at Artemisium, so he now ascended a throne set on a high place across from Salamis. From here he could see the battle and had by his side a group of scribes whose job it was to set down the names of those who performed well or badly. Reward or chastisement would follow in due course.[15]

As we shall soon be in a position to appreciate, this battle was to be one of the most important fought among the Persian invasion and has some claim to be considered to mark the turning point in the war. Yet, for all of that, the accounts which have come down to us are of such a quality that we can only offer a somewhat sketchy, and at times tentative, reconstruction of events.

Map 5: The Battle of Salamis, 480 BC.

The Greeks formed two lines, with those in the second covering the gaps between the ships in the first. The Athenians faced the Phoenicians, the Spartans the Ionians. Most likely next to them were the Corinthians, Aeginetans and Megarians, with the contingent from other Greek states in the centre. As the Persians advanced, the Greeks backed water. We may dismiss the story that an apparition in the shape of a woman called upon them to stop. More credence is to be attached to the report that either an Athenian or Aeginetan vessel – the matter has never been settled – rammed a Persian and began the battle in this way.

In the fight which now ensued, the role of the Corinthians is controversial. The Athenians were to later claim they had played no part in the fighting. As it began, Adeimantus, their commander, sailed off and was followed by the rest of their squadron. They had got to a point on the coast of Salamis where there was a temple of Athena. Here they were met by a boat. From whence it came no-one knew, but the men on board shouted to Adeimantus to turn back, as the Greeks were winning. The Corinthians duly turned around only to find, when they got back, that the battle was over. The Corinthians disputed this and had the agreement and support of the rest of Greece. Independent evidence confirms their contention. The most telling is the inscription on a grave from Attica, which is known to us not only from Greek literature but from actual remains. This records the burial of Corinthian dead, which would not have been done without Athenian consent and would not have been an honour accorded to cowards.

So what, then, lies behind this story? One school of thought believed that Xerxes had sent a squadron of Egyptians to block the strait between the island of Salamis and the Megarid on the mainland opposite. On this view the Corinthians will then have been on a special mission to deal with this threat. This theory seems to go back to Ephorus. We have met with this fourth century BC historian before, when we came upon his theory that the Persians and Carthaginians had acted in concert to attack the Greek world.

We wondered then if this was not the result of misplaced cleverness and ingenuity, and we may wonder again here. The Egyptian foray might very well be simply the product of Ephorus' imagination. But, if we dismiss Ephorus, then we are faced with an explanation which is more sinister than mere invention. In the next generation, Corinth and Athens, once allies, were to be enemies. They took opposite sides in the Peloponnesian War and it was Athenian interference in a quarrel between her and her colony, Corcyra, which helped to bring on this conflict. Thus there is, at the very least, a suspicion that the Athenians put about, then, this slanderous tale.

The only other detailed accounts we have concerning the battle consist of reports of three incidents, all of which seem to have happened as the battle turned against the Persians.

The first of these involved Queen Artemisia. She was pursued by an Athenian trireme. Her escape route was blocked by ships of her own side so, in order to effect her escape – the Athenians had put a price on her head for daring, as a woman, to confront them – she rammed one of the vessels. This went down with all hands so that there was no one to lay information against her. The Athenian thought she was either one of his own or a deserter from the Persians and called off the chase. Xerxes, seeing what had happened and thinking Artemisia had destroyed an enemy ship, exclaimed that his men were turning into women and his women into men.

A group of Phoenicians was not so lucky. They came to Xerxes to complain their ships had been lost due to Ionian treachery. At this moment a ship from Samothrace rammed an Athenian and sank it whereupon an Aeginetan, in turn, sank the Samothracian. Her crew, however, leapt aboard the Aeginetan and, driving her marines from the deck, captured her. Xerxes, seeing all this, flew into a rage and had the heads of the Phoenicians chopped off, as they had slandered brave men.

As the Persians retreated, the Athenians fell upon them in the narrows and such as got clear fell into the hands of the Aeginetans.

At one point Themistocles himself was nearby when an Aeginetan rammed a Sidonian. The Aeginetan was commanded by a man called Polycritus, who was a son of that Crius who had once defied Cleomenes. On this occasion old antagonism between Athenian and Aeginetan briefly manifested itself, when Polycritus shouted at Themistocles, asking if he still thought that the Aeginetans were medizers?

The battle appears to have lasted the whole day. What decided it was the ability of the Greeks to keep their formation, while that of the Persians disintegrated. The greatest damage was done when those who attacked first tried to turn around and became entangled in those who were pressing from behind. Naturally there were casualties on both sides but those of the Persians were heavier since many, who did not know how to swim, drowned, while the Greeks, who did, made it to Salamis. The surviving Persian vessels made it back to Phaleron where they were under the protection of the army. Those on Psyttaleia, however, were slaughtered by a force of hoplites led by Aristides.[16]

The Greeks now towed such of their crippled ships that were still afloat to Salamis. Some wreckage floated to Attica to be used for firewood and some saw in this the fulfilment of an ancient prophecy that the women there would cook with oars. The Greeks did not yet fully appreciate the extent of their victory and expected Xerxes would renew the conflict. He indeed gave signs of doing so. Chief among those was the beginning of the building of a mole in the direction of Salamis which was constructed, like that over the Hellespont, by lashing boats together. But already Xerxes had begun to fear the victorious Greeks would sail there and break them down. Morale had suffered a severe dent. When Athens fell, a courier was despatched with the joyful news to Susa. Now a second was sent to tell of the reversal. The first had been greeted with feasting and rejoicing, the second with wailing and lamentation. In these circumstances, Xerxes began to contemplate flight and escape.

At this point Mardonius waited upon him. He had been forward in advocating the war and, in consequence, had most to gain from success and most to lose from failure therein. He professed himself unfazed by this defeat. The struggle would be settled by campaigns on land and not by sea battles. The successful Greek sailors would not face the Persian army and it should be borne in mind that those overwhelmed at Salamis were from the subject peoples and were not the Persians themselves. He advocated an attack on the Peloponnese, either now or a little later. Should Xerxes decide to pull out, he asked him to leave an army with which he, Mardonius, could complete the conquest of Greece.

Xerxes decided to put Mardonius' advice to a conference but then, as the story has it, remembered Artemisia's sound advice before the battle, so he instead had a private meeting with her. She advocated that Xerxes indeed should quit and leave Mardonius behind. If he prevailed then Xerxes would have the credit because Mardonius, after all, was his slave. If he failed, it didn't much matter and no great harm would come to the king. In any case, Xerxes could take comfort from having achieved one of his great objectives: the destruction of Athens.

No doubt these considerations weighed with Xerxes, but there is something suspicious about this interview. Artemisia and Demaratus were both in a position to give advice and opinion to the king of Persia when asked. What is very doubtful is that they were in any position to sway with such advice and opinion. We doubt if Darius appointed Xerxes king because he was counselled by Demaratus and, in the same way, we doubt if Xerxes' decision to pull out was due to what Artemisia had said to him. Once more we are witnessing the Greek fondness for exaggerating their influence at the Achaemenid court.

Xerxes now told Mardonius to get his army together. The fleet then slipped out of Phaleron and made at speed for the Hellespont. When the Greeks found out, they set off in pursuit. They got as far as Andros, where they stopped for another one of their debates.

Themistocles advocated carrying on with the pursuit. Eurybiades spoke against this and in favour of carrying the war into Asia. If Xerxes were trapped in Greece, he would only carry on the war and his men would continue to devour the substance of the Greek states.

The majority agreed with Eurybiades, and Themistocles not only changed tack but turned the situation to his future advantage. To the Athenians, who had been his strong supporters when he advocated destruction, he said it was always dangerous to challenge a cornered man. Thanks to the gods, the man who had profaned their temples was now in flight and the time was come for them to look after their own interests. The Hellespont and Asia could wait until next year. Once he had soothed his audience, Themistocles summoned the faithful Sicinnus and sent him with another message to Xerxes, who was still with the army in Attica. He told him to say to the king that Themistocles, though a Greek leader, had persuaded his fellow countrymen not to sail to the Hellespont.

Those who doubt the historicity of Themistocles' first piece of mendacity are even more troubled by this second example. Yet doubts are, I believe, otiose. No man can exactly foretell the future, but the shrewd Themistocles was resolved to ensure his own. He knew Athenian politics better than we ever can, but we see what he clearly saw, the primary lesson to be learned from the vicissitudes of life in a democracy: today one could be the darling of the people, tomorrow the object of its hatred. He himself had engineered the exile of Aristides and even more, I suggest, he will have thought of Miltiades, one year the hero of Marathon, the next a broken defendant before a law court. People like Demaratus and the Pisistratids showed clearly Persia could offer a place of refuge to the exile. Some years later what Themistocles dimly foresaw happened, and he had to run from Greece with a price on his head. But he was able to call in the favour and convince the king that the good he had done Persia outweighed the bad, so that he was kindly received by his old foes.[17]

Now the Greeks laid siege to Andros to punish her for medizing and Themistocles took this opportunity to try and extract money from the islanders. He told them he had the backing of two powerful deities, Persuasion and Compulsion. Entering into the spirit of the thing, the Andrians replied that, while their gods obviously brought the Athenians prosperity, they themselves were a poor people in thrall to two other deities, Poverty and Inability, and they were unable to get rid of them. They, therefore, did not propose to pay and so the siege went on. Themistocles sent messengers round to the other islands, also to demand money. Carystus and Paros paid up, knowing what was going on at Andros. The Parians, in this way, went unscathed, but the Carystians still had their territory ravaged. The other commanders are said to have been in ignorance of these transactions, but Herodotus suspected Themistocles also tried to squeeze money out of other islands. One other attempt at extortion did come to light because of the victim Themistocles picked on. A certain Timocreon of Rhodes had been banished for medizing. Themistocles promised to have him restored in return for a bribe, but then reneged on the deal. Unfortunately Timocreon was a poet and attacked Themistocles as a money grubber, in verses which were widely circulated, and grew even more abusive when Themistocles was later forced in to exile.

There are those who have been troubled by these stories. What at base lies at their reaction is a reluctance to accept that a national hero could be less than perfect and that he could not display weakness in any department. Some historians, too, have expressed doubts and wonder if we are looking at slanders put about by Themistocles' many enemies. These writers appear to have been influenced by the fact that today we, almost instinctively, require high standards of those whom we elect to high office. But they forget two things. Even today such people can, on occasion, disappoint us and in times past the standards people expected were simply not as high. If we want to understand Themistocles we need to think of such figures as Clive of India and bear ever in mind that he was simply indulging in the practices of his age.

After the demonstration in the islands, the Greek fleet returned to Salamis. Here they took from among the plunder certain objects to be dedicated to the gods in thanksgiving. Next they divided the plunder among themselves but reserved a part for Delphi. Upon enquiry the god said he was generally satisfied with what he had got but demanded more of the Aeginetans, who then sent a bronze mast dedicated with stars to Delphi. Then the Greeks made for the Isthmus. Work on the wall had temporarily halted, as Cleombrotus, the Spartan commander, had marched his army home after receiving an ill omen. As we shall see in the next chapter, it was to be resumed in 479 BC. For the moment, though, our attention is drawn to the attempt by the Greeks to decide who should win the prize for valour.

There was general agreement that the Aeginetans had as a state earned this. When it came to decide which individual should be so awarded, large egos went on display. By now the reader will have become acquainted with some of the admirable traits of the Greek character such as courage, which manifested itself above all at Thermopylae. The aftermath of that battle certainly brought home to Xerxes the quality of the people he was warring with. On the day after, some Arcadians came to his camp. They were interrogated and asked what the Greeks were doing and replied they were celebrating the Olympic Games. They added that the prizes in the contests were wreaths of olive. One of the Persians present, on hearing this, exclaimed to Mardonius that he had been responsible for bringing them to fight men who only competed for honour. About the same time, Achaemenes, a brother of Xerxes, showed he was fully aware of a less attractive side of the Greek character. It will be recalled that, after the battle, Xerxes had also asked Demaratus' advice on how the Peloponnese might best be subdued and that Achaemenes had intervened in the discussion. He reminded his brother that Demaratus was a Greek and that as a people they envied the good luck of others and hated those who were faring better than themselves.

This begrudging attitude now manifested itself, as each captain nominated himself for the prize for valour, although the majority were prepared to vote the second place to Themistocles. As a result of this display of mean-mindedness, no prize was awarded and everybody sailed home for the winter. The Spartans alone came well out of this. Themistocles visited them shortly after. There Eurybiades was awarded a wreath of olive for his valour, but Themistocles also received one in recognition of his cleverness. In addition, he received a splendid chariot and, on his departure, was given an escort of picked warriors to the border.[18]

At this point there comes an anti-climax. Although Themistocles was to play a part in the reconstruction of Athens in the years which followed, we hear no more of him in this war. Some think his pro-Spartan stance would have made him unpopular at Athens. Further there was to be a change of strategy in 479 BC. In that year the main battle would have to be fought on land and so there would be much less need of Themistocles' talents. All of this could mean he failed to be elected to office. On the other hand, this very lack of need for his particular skills might just mean that, though in fact elected, he had no opportunity to show what he could do. Much of this naturally is speculation, but what is fact is that in 479 BC Aristides commanded the Athenian army, while Xanthippus had charge of the fleet.

Yet, I believe it would be wrong to end on this anti-climactic note, and rather record the esteem the common people of Greece held him in. At the next Olympic Games, when Themistocles came into the stadium, everybody stopped looking at the competitions and turned to gaze upon the architect of the victory.[19]

In the meanwhile, Xerxes had quitted Attica and marched into Boeotia with his army. Mardonius accompanied him and, when the army got to Thessaly, he chose from it the men whom he wished to have with him for the next year's campaigning. There were chiefly

Persians, Medes, Sacae, Bactrians and Indians, and the intent was to winter here, as the season was now well advanced. While Xerxes was still in Thessaly, a delegation arrived from the Spartans to demand satisfaction for the death of Leonidas. In parenthesis we may remark that this recalls the demand to Cyrus to leave the Asiatic Greeks alone. Spartans were never over-awed by Persian kings. Xerxes simply laughed and said Mardonius would give them the satisfaction they wanted. We shall see in our next chapter that this promise was fulfilled, but not in the way Xerxes will have intended.

Xerxes now made his way through Thessaly towards his final destination, the Bosphorus. Supplies had failed and the troops were reduced to eating grass, leaves and the bark of trees. With such a diet, it comes as no surprise to learn that plague and dysentery spread among them. Numbers had to be left behind in towns in Thessaly itself, but also in Paeonia and Macedon, as they passed through those lands. At last the army made it to Thrace and the Bosphorus. Here the Persians found the bridges were down, destroyed not by the Greeks but by storms. An alternative version has it that Xerxes himself only went as far as Eion on the Strymon and left it to Hydarnes to lead the army across to Abydus. He then took ship only to encounter a great storm. The captain told him the ship could be saved only if the load was lightened. Xerxes called for volunteers and a number of Persian nobles came forward, made obeisance and jumped into the sea. When they made it to harbour, Xerxes gave the captain a gold crown for saving his life and then had his head removed because he had caused the death of so many Persians.

Not all accept this version of events but it can be believed that, when the army got safely across, its troubles were not ended. Finding an abundance of food at Abydus after the dearth on the march, many of the men gorged themselves and perished in consequence.

Part of Mardonius' force was detached to escort Xerxes safely to the Bosphorus. It was under the command of a Persian noble called Artabazus, who was destined to play a prominent part in the remainder of the war. On the way back to Mardonius, he laid siege to Potidea which, once it had seen Xerxes' retreat, had risen in revolt. He also turned on Olynthus since he had suspicions of the townsfolk's intention. He killed them all and chucked the bodies into a nearby lake. He was not so successful at Potidea. Troops from Scione stiffened its garrison but their commander, Timoxenus, decided to betray the town. He and Artabazus communicated by shooting arrows with messages attached to each other. Unfortunately one went astray and the plot was discovered by the townsfolk. They took no action against Timoxenus but the siege went on. Some three months after, there was a very low tide on the peninsula on which the town stood. The Persians crossed over, thinking to take advantage of this, but then the waters rose again unexpectedly. Many were drowned as they could not swim and the remainder were killed by the townsfolk. After this Artabazus seems to have decided it was pointless to continue, so he marched off to rejoin Mardonius.[20]

With this, fighting stopped for the year 480 BC and so it is time for us to briefly review the situation and this may best be done by reference to the three great battles of that year and their consequences. Thermopylae had militarily been a disaster and had left central Greece open to the Persians. But it had also proved to be inspirational as it offered a lesson in heroic self-sacrifice. Artemisium may be described as indecisive and, as we saw from the debates before Salamis, had not completely confirmed the Greeks in their confidence in their ability to face the enemy on the sea, their natural element. Salamis was the decisive battle. In the first instance, it drove the Persian navy out of the waters of mainland Greece, and ensured that it would no longer be the aggressor but would have to stand on the defensive in a conflict which would take place in Asia Minor. In the second place, it led Xerxes to pull part of his land forces out of Greece. It is true that a large Persian force remained and that it still had the support of its medizing Greek allies, but its morale was badly shaken. Salamis was not the end but it brought that end closer, an end which was to come in the next year at a great land battle.

Chapter 7

Mycale and Plataea (479 BC)

With the ending of winter and the start, once more, of the sailing season, the Greek fleet again moved abroad. In the spring of 479 BC it proceeded to Aegina under the command of the Spartan Leotychides. Here it received a delegation. This had originated in Chios. Its members had tried to overthrow the tyrant ruler there. When this had failed its members had gone to Sparta to ask the Spartans to liberate Ionia. These now directed the request to Leotychides. Although there were many of the more adventurous Athenians in the allied fleet, habitual Spartan caution won out and the Greeks went no further than Delos. On the other side, the Persians, plainly demoralized by their defeat at Salamis, would not venture beyond Samos. So, for some months, there was stalemate and a standoff.

Eventually (August 479 BC) this stalemate was broken. Another delegation, this time from Samos, waited upon Leotychides and repeated the earlier request saying Ionia was indeed now ready to revolt. This time the Spartan commander bestirred himself and the fleet sailed for Samos. Morale among the Persians continued to be low and, at the approach of the Greeks, they retreated to Mycale on the mainland opposite Samos where, it will be recalled, the Panionion used to meet.

On a headland here they beached their ships and constructed a fort of wood and stone. The Greeks first sailed along the shore and, as they did so, they called out to the Ionians in the Persian army to desert. They next put ashore at some distance from their enemy and made ready to give battle. The Persians saw what was happening and made preparations of their own. First of all, they disarmed the Samians of whom they had now, not unnaturally, begun to conceive suspicions. Next they sent the Milesians to guard the passes into the hills behind Mycale. Finally, they themselves left the protection of their fort and formed a shield wall before it.

The Greek line stretched from the water's edge up to some hills. The Athenians together with the Corinthians and others advanced along the beach itself but the extended line meant the Spartans had to advance up a gully and into those hills. In consequence, their advance was slower and the Athenians thus first came into contact with the enemy. The Persians made great resistance but the Greeks finally broke the shield wall and forced them back into their fort. The Greeks, however, burst in here and, with the arrival of the Spartans, at last overcame the foe even though isolated groups of Persians fought to the last. Their commander Tigranes was killed. Some managed to get away into the hills but there the Milesians turned on them. They led them astray and brought them back among the enemy and then themselves joined in the killing. Finally the Greeks looted the Persian fort and ships before setting fire to both.

As a result of this battle Ionia now rose against Persia for the second time. The Greeks next sailed back to Samos where they began to consider what was to be done. The Spartans revived an idea which, it may be remembered, some had proposed at the time of the Ionian revolt, namely that the Ionians should abandon Asia Minor altogether. The lands of the medizers would provide for them. The Athenians, presuming on their position as the mother of Ionia, would have none of it and it was finally decided that Samos, Lesbos, Chios and the other islands should join the alliance and swear the oath of allegiance. This done, the entire force sailed to the Hellespont to destroy the bridges only to discover, as Xerxes had done the previous year, that they were already down.

The Spartans now wanted to go home but the Athenian contingent under Xanthippus elected to stay and laid siege to

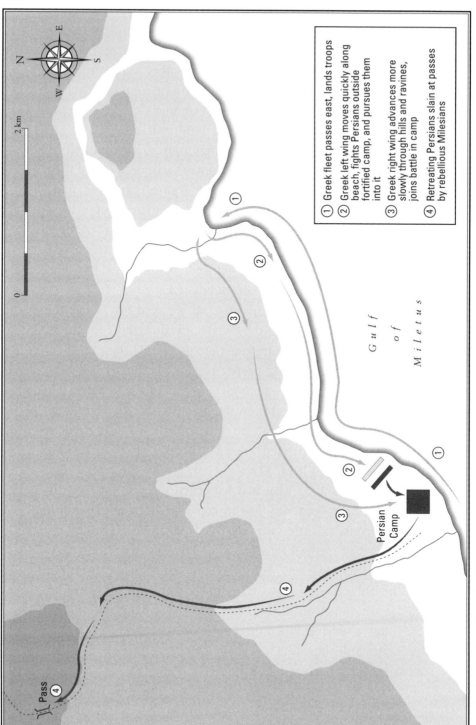

1. Greek fleet passes east, lands troops
2. Greek left wing moves quickly along beach, fights Persians outside fortified camp, and pursues them into it
3. Greek right wing advances more slowly through hills and ravines, joins battle in camp
4. Retreating Persians slain at passes by rebellious Milesians

Gulf of Miletus

Persian Camp

Pass

2 km

Map 6: The Battle of Mycale, 479 BC.

Sestus in the Chersonese. The town's defences were strong but provisions were scarce. Nonetheless the town held out until well on into the winter. One evening the Persian commanders Artaÿces and Oeabazus slipped out and the town surrendered.

Oeabazus evaded his Greek pursuers only to be captured by some Thracians who made of him a human sacrifice to one of their gods. Artaÿces was captured and met arguably an even more gruesome end. He had contrived to loot the tomb of a hero, Protesilaus, and had sex with women there. This was sacrilege demanding retribution. Artaÿces tried to retrieve the situation with an enormous bribe but it was refused. Xanthippus had him crucified and stoned his son to death before his eyes.[1]

These were important campaigns and we need not labour the point. But, for the ending of the Persian invasion, those fought on the Greek mainland that same year were more important.

Even before campaigning proper began, Mardonius had been busy and once more the religious element enters our narrative. He sent a Carian called Mys around the oracular shrines. Herodotus says he did not know what he was looking for but modern commentators are prepared to speculate he may have been seeking reassurance since on land, as on the sea, morale must have been damaged as a result of what had happened the previous year. In fact, it may have been very low in some quarters, as something which happened a little later clearly demonstrates. One of the leading Theban medizers invited some Persians to a banquet. As they drank afterwards one of the Persians seemed to have overdone it – as he had tears in his eyes as he spoke. Turning to a Theban he, with the maudlin gloom of the drunk, assured him that few of them were going to survive. When the Theban said he should say that to Mardonius, his companion said it was a matter of Fate but that they dare say nothing to their commander.

That commander's next move was to try and split the Greek alliance. This had, as we know, worked in the past and Mardonius evidently thought it worth trying again, especially as he probably knew that all was not well between Athens and Sparta. So he despatched an agent to Athens. The man he chose was Alexander of Macedon who had played, and was to play again, an ambiguous role in events. He brought with him rather attractive terms. The Athenians could have their territory back and add to it if they wished. Their temples would be rebuilt and they could govern themselves in any way they wished. All they had to do was to acknowledge Xerxes as their master. Alexander added that he personally advised acceptance as this was the best deal they could expect.

For a moment there was perhaps a danger the Athenians might listen to this because they were now becoming irked with Sparta. The Spartans seemed to be reverting to their policy of defending the Peloponnese and letting the rest of Greece fall into Persian hands. In fact they were, at that very moment, completing the building of the wall across the Isthmus of Corinth, begun in the previous year. But, for all of the narrowness of this policy, they clearly did not want to see Athens medize. So they sent a delegation at the same time as Alexander's mission. These ambassadors appealed to the Athenian sense of honour. On a more practical note they offered to provide for all Athenian women and children as long as the war should last. They counselled the Athenians not to be taken in by the charmer Alexander.

The Athenians were not, in fact, taken in and sent Alexander on his way, warning him not to return. However, they also had a message for Sparta. They were very grateful for the offer of help for non-combatants but this was not enough. They expected to see the Spartan army on the march without delay.

When his terms were rejected, Mardonius immediately set his army in motion. Ignoring a Theban request to remain in Boeotia, he pushed on to Athens and took it for a second time but, once more, the Athenians had taken refuge in Salamis. The Persian commander now made overtures again and repeated his generous offer. Once more he was rebuffed and an Athenian councillor who suggested they might be discussed in the assembly was lynched along with his family.

Still the Spartans showed no disposition to stir and, in exasperation, the Athenians sent ambassadors to remonstrate. Pointed reference was made to the attractive Persian offer and to the fact that they had rejected it. The Athenians had behaved nobly while the Spartans had done nothing save lurk behind the Isthmus. For a fortnight the Spartans made no reply but kept the Athenian delegation waiting, saying they were celebrating yet another festival. At last the Athenians had had enough and told their hosts they proposed to compound with Xerxes. Then the Spartans sprung their surprise and said an army was already on the road to the Isthmus commanded by the regent Pausanias.[2]

Hitherto the Argives have played no part in our story. Though they had medized they were tucked away in the Peloponnese and saw no action. Now Mardonius set them a task and they failed him. They were to stop the Spartans but in the event could do nothing to halt their march. All they could do was tell Mardonius that the Spartans were coming.

On getting the news, Mardonius wrecked what was left of Athens. He then pulled back to Boeotia which had two advantages from his point of view. He would be near his chief ally Thebes and the plain of Boeotia would be ideal for cavalry. On the way he despatched a force against Megara to confront a Greek advance guard which had already penetrated this far. He himself led the rest of the army by way of Decelea and Tanagra before occupying a position on the northern side of the Asopus River. Here he built a fort of wood.

As he gathered further forces something curious occurred. Among those who came in was a force of Phocian infantry. They were ordered to form up on open ground. Then Mardonius had his cavalry surround them. These threw some spears but the Phocians held firm and they withdrew. Quite why Mardonius did this is not clear. Some were prepared to believe that the Thessalians, traditional foes of the Phocians, had put Mardonius up to this. Or it may be that he himself suspected them of being reluctant medizers and wished to test them.[3]

Meantime the Spartans had got as far as the Isthmus where they were joined by other contingents from the Peloponnese. They then advanced on Eleusis and were soon joined by the Athenians. Together they moved to the Asopus. There they took up a position at Erythrae, on the slopes of Mount Cithaeron, on the opposite side of the river from the enemy.

As the Greeks showed no inclination to move from this advantageous position, Mardonius sent his cavalry to dislodge them. They were commanded by a man called Masistius who was clad in magnificent heavy armour. The Persians attacked in waves and, as they did so, they hurtled their worst insult at the Greeks, for they shouted they were nothing but women. More seriously they hard pressed their opponents. The Megarians bore the brunt of the assault here and sent to Pausanias for aid as they could not resist much longer. Pausanias called for volunteers and the Athenians responded. They sent a force which contained archers. The Persians continued to attack until Masistius' horse was felled. Because of his heavy armour he could not get up but that same armour protected him until one of the Greeks struck him a blow with a javelin to the eye, where he was vulnerable. Seeing their chief fall, the Persians charged again to recover his body and a great struggle began. The Athenians were able to call on more reinforcements and drive them off. The Persian cavalry retired to their own lines while the Greeks paraded Masistius' body in a wagon before their own troops. This was done in no spirit of derision or triumphalism. Rather, it highlights a facet of the Greek character. They were ever fascinated by male beauty and physical perfection and, even though it was in death, they wished to gaze upon this handsome man.

We can see that the Greek position was a strong one but it had one great weakness, shortage of water. So Pausanias resolved to move in order to be nearer the Gargaphian spring. This was in the territory of the Plataeans and in order to reach it the army marched past Hysiae along the lower slopes of Cithaeron.

When the Greek forces had come together at Eleusis they had sworn an oath to remain loyal to each other and to fight to the death against the Persians. In spite of this, as the army took up its new position, there now occurred another of those unseemly squabbles among the Greeks which punctuated these wars. This one arose over who should have the secondmost place of honour on the left wing for the most honourable, on the right, was reserved for the Spartans. The dispute was between the Tegeans and the Athenians. Both sides made appeal to a mixture of legend, history and recent events. The Tegeans pointed out that they had always had this position when the Peloponnesians went to war in recognition of the wars they had fought for and against Sparta. The Athenians then recounted some of their legendary exploits in the Peloponnese and against the mythic women warriors, the Amazons, before drawing attention to the most telling detail of all. They had already defeated the Persians at Marathon. The decision was left to the Spartans and by acclamation they declared the position should go to the Athenians. Between the two wings were placed the other Greek contingents from Tegea, Corinth, Potidea, Orchomenus, Sicyon, Epidaurus, Troezen, Lepreum, Mycenae, Phlius, Hermion, Eretria, Chalcis, Ambrocia, Leucos, Paleous, Aegina, Megara and, finally, Plataea.

Mardonius followed in the wake of the enemy and positioned his lines opposite. He placed his Persians facing the Spartans. The Medes, Bactrians and Sacae faced the other Greeks except for the Athenians who were opposed by the medizing Greeks in the Persian army.

For eight days neither side made a move. Both employed Greek diviners and these after sacrifice gave the same advice: defence would be successful but attack disastrous. Pausanias may have been untroubled by this hiatus. Reinforcements were still coming in and it was obviously good to have available the greatest number when the battle proper started. But a pause such as this, with its attendant idleness, brings its own dangers. Among the Athenian contingent a conspiracy began. Some young men began to plot to overthrow the democracy and give aid to the Persians. If we place this firmly in its historical context we can easily see how it happened. Marathon had revealed the existence of a pro–Persian anti-democratic element in Athens and there is no reason to suppose it ever went away, even though unity had been maintained up to this. As proof of this we may recall the councillor who had suggested Xerxes' terms be accepted and was lynched for his plans. Those who schemed now belonged to some of the richest families in the city and it was but natural they should be of an oligarchic temper. Their present circumstances had served to sharpen that temper. All Athenians had lost much, when the Persians took and destroyed their city, but they had lost most.

The plot seems to have already won a fair number of adherents in the camp itself, when it came to the attention of Aristides, who was now commander of the Athenian contingent and who dealt with it in a most skilful manner. Some modern scholars, who have no experience and still less appreciation of the realities of military life, insist that commanders should always proceed with great severity against mutiny and unrest in the ranks and deplore it when this does not happen. Aristides was a real soldier and knew different. The situation called for subtlety and finesse. He arrested just eight of the plotters and formally accused them of treachery. Two managed to escape and Aristides released the rest without proceeding further against them. He told them that they could purge their guilt by fighting bravely in the battle which was soon to come.

On the eighth day Mardonius made a move. Acting on the advice of a Theban who knew the country well, he despatched that evening a force to the passes of Cithaeron to block the supply line of the Greeks and prevent further reinforcements reaching them. Almost immediately a success was scored when a supply train was intercepted and destroyed.

For the next two days the Persian cavalry rode up to the banks of the Asopus to provoke their opponents but when the Greek horse approached they rode off without engaging. On the tenth day

Mardonius decided something would have to be done to end the standoff, so he took counsel with his chief subordinate, Artabazus. Artabazus gave it as his opinion that they should withdraw and hole up in Thebes. Now, it is virtually an axiom that to stand on the defensive means one cannot win a war and, indeed, greatly increases the risk of defeat. Artabazus, though, claimed that his strategy would work here. There was an abundance of supplies for man and beast in Thebes and thus the Persians could withstand a long siege. Given the Greeks' lack of skill in this kind of warfare, it was unlikely they would be able to take the town. As they lay before it, dissensions would inevitably occur among them and the second part of Artabazus' plan could then be put into operation. The Persians also had abundant supplies of coin, and once this had been distributed among the restless, the opposition alliance would fall apart. Mardonius, however, would have none of this but declared he was determined on giving battle where he was and that it would be on the very next day.

His plans were revealed to the Greeks by that ambiguous man, Alexander of Macedon. He, it will be recalled, was later to cloak his initial act of medism by pretending to have murdered the Persian envoys, and had played a hazardous and exciting part in this war, flitting between both sides in order to garner a store of goodwill with whoever might win. We have already seen him advise the Greeks at Tempe but also act as Mardonius' ambassador to Athens. Now, he was set on storing up merit for himself with the Greeks. Under the cover of night he sneaked across to the Athenian sentries. Mardonius had chosen him to go to Athens because of his good relations with the Athenians. So, he here capitalized on these relations in order to get a favourable reception. He told them that the omens for the Persians still continued to be bad but that Mardonius had determined to ignore them and go over to the attack. If, however, that attack did not come, then the Greeks should stay where they were because Mardonius only had food for a few days more. He pompously declared that he was acting out of

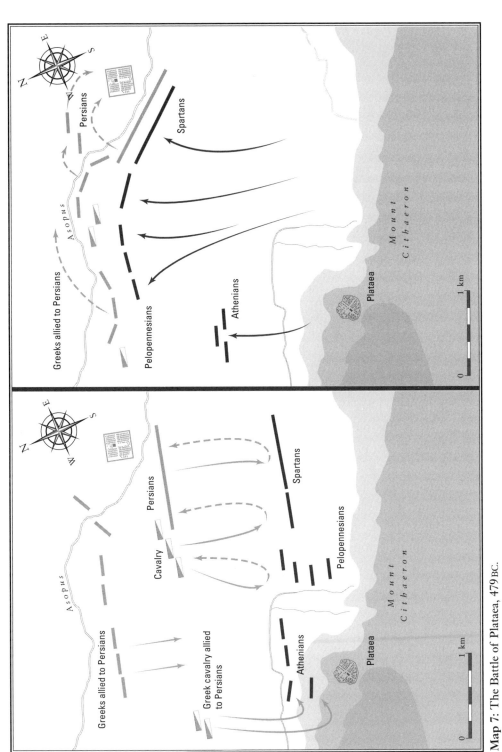

Map 7: The Battle of Plataea, 479 BC.

his love for Greece and his desire to save her from slavery. His next remark was grounded on a more practical consideration and was very revealing. Should the Greeks win, he hoped they would remember his services and be able to do something for him.

When Alexander had ridden off into the night, the sentries reported what he had said to their officers, who then informed Pausanias. He, in the light of what he had heard, took a tactical decision. As the Athenians had already at Marathon experience of dealing with the Persians, he decided to switch them to the right wing. The Spartans, who had never defeated Persians, would then go to the left where they would face the medizing Greeks whom they would be more than able to deal with. Mardonius, however, spotted what was going on and simply moved his Persians to the other wing, so that they still faced the Spartans. Pausanias next put his Spartans on the right wing and Mardonius again did the same, so that in the end everybody wound up being where they had been in the first place, before the arabesque began.

After this piece of futile manoeuvring, Mardonius decided he would try to provoke the Spartans. He sent out a herald to taunt them. This man declared they were cowards unable to face the Persians and leaving it to Athenians to fight them. He proposed a group of Persians and Spartans should fight it out. Whoever won would decide the outcome of the war unless, of course, the remaining troops on either side then wanted to fight.

One can only imagine the reaction of these great warriors to this sort of thing, but they held themselves in and did not deign to reply. Once more Mardonius sent his cavalry against the Greeks. These with their arrows and javelins did severe damage and further managed to work their way around the Greeks to block up and foul the Gargaphian spring from which the Greeks drew most of their water.

Pausanias' officers now waited upon him. They pointed not only to this problem with water but to the fact that food supplies were also running low thanks to the Persian operations at the passes from

Cithaeron. It was therefore resolved to move and make for a place called 'the Island', near the River Oëroe and Plataea.

For the rest of the day the Greeks stayed where they were even though they had to endure constant harassment by the enemy cavalry. When night fell these attacks ceased and the bulk of the army, which comprised the centre, began its march. Later malicious tradition was to represent this as something of a disorganized rout which culminated in the army forming a scattered encampment around Plataea. The truth is otherwise. The soldiers had set out at the time agreed and made an orderly march. Even if they never reached their primary objective of 'the Island', they were now in a place from which they were able to protect the supply trains coming from the passes in Cithaeron.

Once the main body of his army was on the move, Pausanias decided it was time for the Spartans, Tegeans and Athenians on the wings to follow. This was when trouble began. Pausanias gave the order to the Spartans to march but Amompharetus, a divisional commander, would not budge. This man is almost a caricature of the ancient Spartan. Tough and stubborn and of undoubted courage, he did not intend to run away from anybody but determined to stand and fight the Persians where he stood. In his refusal to desert his post he bears a certain resemblance to Leonidas but what could be lauded as heroic self-sacrifice at Thermopylae could be castigated as stupidity at Plataea.

Fearing that Amompharetus' attitude would mean the destruction of him and his men, Pausanias countermanded his orders and went to try and reason with him. The Athenians by now had become puzzled at the Spartan failure to stir so they sent over someone to find out what was going on. This messenger arrived to find that Pausanias and Amompharetus were still arguing. Pausanias told the emissary the Athenians should move closer to the Spartans and be ready to follow them.

When day dawned the wrangling between Pausanias and his subordinate was still continuing but by now the situation was serious indeed. The night march had been conceived in order to escape the harassment of the Persian cavalry and, with light, that would now begin again. Pausanias decided that he had had enough of Amompharetus and his antics. So he left him where he was and began to march at the head of the Spartans and Tegeans and was accompanied by the Athenians. He appears to have calculated that, once he saw everybody else leaving, Amompharetus would move too. If he made that calculation he was correct. When Amompharetus saw that Pausanias was in earnest, he now followed and the Spartans then waited for him to catch up.

The Spartans and the Tegeans marched along the foothills of Cithaeron while the Athenians went by way of a lower road on the plain. Mardonius was by this time watching but could only see the Spartans and the Tegeans since the Athenians were hidden from his view, thanks to the route they had taken. He paused to allow himself the luxury of making a few more disparaging remarks about the Spartans to some of the medizing Greeks in his entourage. Yesterday, he said, they had tried to get out of line to avoid facing the Persians and now they were simply running away. Plainly their reputation was somewhat exaggerated.

The cavalry of the Persians had by now started to harass the Spartans once more and Mardonius gave orders to his Persian contingent to cross the river, and they were closely followed by the remainder of the army who are said to have advanced in no particular order.

By this time the harrying of the cavalry had become so severe that Pausanias sent a message to the Athenians who had now reached 'the Island', imploring them to come to his assistance. They, though, could do nothing for him as they themselves now faced a heavy attack from the medizing Greeks. Pausanias with his Spartans and Tegeans would have to look out for himself.

With their work completed, the Persian cavalry now gave way and allowed the infantry to engage. As at Mycale, they set up a shield wall from which they rained down arrows on their enemies. Even in this situation the Spartans did not lose sight of their religious obligations but made sacrifice to obtain an omen. This proved unfavourable and Pausanias prayed to heaven. Then the Tegeans, growing impatient, gave a shout and sprang to the attack, at which moment, we are assured, the omens turned out favourable. The fight was carried to the shield wall and, after a great struggle, this was broken. But even then the struggle continued for as long as Mardonius, conspicuous on a white horse, lived. Eventually he was felled – hit by a stone thrown by a Spartan in one account – perishing together with his bodyguard. At this point Persian resistance collapsed and the survivors fled to their fort. The Spartans pursued and laid siege to the place.

Meantime things had not been turning out too well for the Athenians. Most of the medizing Greeks do not seem to have fought well, but the Thebans and Boeotians were an exception. In the fourth century BC their infantry were to be the best in Greece and their ancestors here put up a great resistance. Their cavalry, too, impressed and inflicted severe damage on a Megarian contingent which had come to stiffen Athenian resistance. News of the victory of Pausanias broke up the fight here. The Thebans and their allies retreated in good order with the cavalry providing effective cover. They did not head for the Persian fort but made their way back to their own city.

All this time the Spartans were trying to break into the Persian fort, but without success. Now the Athenians arrived and the Greeks succeeded in making a breach through which they charged. Indiscriminate slaughter and looting then followed.

Pausanias gave orders that all of the loot should be collected by the helots. One must regretfully record that they succeeded in making off with some of it for themselves. They did not, though, know the value of much of what they had pilfered for, supposing gold to be brass, they sold it cheaply to the Aeginetans who were perfectly well aware of what they were getting.

What the helots had not siphoned off was still a great amount. A tenth was now dedicated to the shrine at Delphi. From this various statues were made. One of the trophies created then survives to this day, as we noted in our last chapter. In the Hippodrome in Istanbul may still be seen part of the column which had three serpents' heads and on which were inscribed the names of those Greek states who had defeated the Persians. The rest of the booty was distributed fairly among the troops. Two states did not share: Mantinea and Elis. Their men arrived too late to take part and, unlike the Spartans at Marathon, had no good excuse. They were packed off home and, when they got there, their officers were exiled on suspicion of medism. They had, it was thought, deliberately marched slowly.

Among those who had fought there was disagreement as to who should receive the prize for valour, as there had been after Salamis. The Athenians would not concede this to the Spartans. Aristides proved to be a restraining influence and, at his urging, the matter was set before the Greeks as a whole. A compromise was reached when the prize was given to the Plataeans.

In victory Pausanias' behaviour was not only proper but chivalrous and, in this, he contrasted strongly with that of Xerxes after Thermopylae. A woman clad in finery made her way to him from among the Persians. Clasping Pausanias' knees in supplication, she told him she was a Greek who had been an unwilling concubine of a Persian grandee. Pausanias assured her she had nothing to fear and arranged for her to be taken, at her own wish, to Aegina. He was also approached by a man from the island called Lampon. He praised Pausanias and the Spartans for what they had done. He then made a proposal. Xerxes had cut off Leonidas' head and impaled it on a spear. Now Pausanias should do the same to Mardonius' body. Pausanias in reply thanked him for his words of praise but added that what he suggested had undone them. No Spartan would behave in such a barbarous fashion. He then ordered Lampon out of his sight.

The booty obtained from the Persians had been rich indeed. Gold and silver was to be had in abundance. What especially attracted attention, though, were Mardonius' personal possessions.

It was especially remarked upon that his horse had a manger made of bronze. His tent, too, was rich with carpets and decorated with precious metals. Viewing it gave Pausanias an idea. Summoning Mardonius' bakers and cooks, he ordered them to prepare a meal such as they would have set before their late master while, at the same time, he ordered his own to make ready a typical Spartan dinner. As he contemplated the magnificence of one and the plainness of the other – even among the ancients, Spartan food had the reputation of being fairly disgusting – Pausanias pointedly remarked that the Persians had been fools when, as men of wealth, they had come to make war on poor men such as themselves.

One part of the Persian army managed to escape. It was commanded by that Artabazus who had advised Mardonius not to give battle. Just where he was positioned on the field is not clear, but what he did is not in dispute. As the other Persians advanced in a disorderly fashion, he ordered his men to keep good order and follow his orders strictly. Plainly they had some ground to cover and, by the time they were ready to engage, the rout had begun. So Artabazus turned about and made straight for Phocis. From here he moved swiftly into Thessaly where he was well received. News of Plataea had not reached here but Artabazus obviously felt he had to give his hosts some explanation as to why he was here, in order to allay any suspicions they might have. He told them he was on a special mission and would soon be followed by Mardonius with the bulk of the army. He then proceeded through Thessaly and Macedonia into Thrace. As with almost everybody else who crossed here, Artabazus received something of a mauling at the hands of the Thracians. Despite this and suffering hunger and exhaustion, Artabazus made it to Byzantium from where he was able to ship his army across to Asia.[4]

With this we witness the end of the Persian invasion. They still held some places in northern Greece, but they were never again to go on the offensive. The Greeks had driven the invader from their country.

Epilogue

With the victory at Plataea, the thoughts of the Greek allies inevitably turned towards punishing those who had medized. Thebes was the first and natural target. Its role had been prominent and it lay close by. So, ten days after the battle, the victors marched on Thebes. Arriving there, they demanded the surrender of those responsible for the pro-Persian policy and they sought especially two men, Attiganus and Timagenidas. When the request was declined, siege was laid to the town and the surrounding countryside was ravaged. This went on for twenty days until Timagenidas addressed his fellow Thebans.

He told them it was clear the siege would go on until Thebes surrendered or the medizers were handed over. It might very well be, though, that all they wanted was money and, if that were the case, then what they asked might be met with from the public purse. If, however, they wanted him and his friends, they were prepared to surrender and face the accusations made against them. The Thebans duly handed the medizers over. In the confusion Attiganus managed to slip away but left his children behind. When they fell into Pausanias' hands, he continued to play the chivalrous part. He did them no harm as they were not answerable for their father's transgressions. The other medizers looked forward to a trial, as they hoped to get away by bribing the judges. Pausanias knew what they were thinking and simply took them away to Corinth, where he had them executed.[1]

After this initial display of vigour, enthusiasm for punishing medizers waned a little. The principal consideration seems to have been the actual difficulty of mounting campaigns which might be prolonged. The main problem was the conducting of sieges. The Greeks at this time were not masters of siegecraft and indeed it was not until the fourth century BC that another tyrant of Syracuse, Dionysius I, devised effective siege machinery. Cities, well supplied with victuals, could easily withstand a siege, and then what Artabazus had recognized full well would happen: attacking armies would just fall apart.

The strength of the places to be attacked had always to be considered. Thebes had handed over the medizers. It had not been taken. And, if there was small hope there, what hope would there be at Argos? And Syracuse? Even if it were acceptable to attack Gelon, who had become a hero for his defeat of the Carthaginians, Syracuse was a great power and not to be lightly provoked. Athens was to do so later in the century and the result was a great disaster.

There was now not an atmosphere of sunny reconciliation and general forgiveness, but of reluctant realism. This may best be illustrated by reference to two incidents. Corcyra's claim that adverse winds had prevented her joining in the campaign was accepted. A Spartan suggestion that medizers be ejected from the Amphictyonic League – the body which oversaw Delphi – was not agreed to, as this would make her influence there too great.

But this did not mean there was an end to campaigning. In 477 BC the medizers were driven from Phocis and part of Thessaly. The Aleudae, who had been the most prominent and vigorous on the Persian side there, managed to survive. They compounded with the Spartans, having given a bribe to their commander.[2]

Meantime, on the sea the allies had conquered part of Cyprus and captured Byzantium. But the most significant event was a meeting in 478 BC, on the flagship of Aristides. The Ionians and Athenians came together to form a League to fight Persia. In the next year (477 BC) this League was formally established with an exchange of oaths. Dubbed the Delian League because its headquarters were established on this island which had sacred associations for both Athens and the Ionians, it now continued the war with Persia.

This war continued until 449 BC when hostilities ceased, possibly – the matter is disputed – with a formal treaty known as the Peace of Callias. By this time, the League had changed its character. It was no longer an alliance. Athens had become dominant and the other states were now her subjects. This mini-empire was viewed with suspicion and distrust by many of the other Greek states, sentiments which eventually led to war between the Athenians on the one side, and the Spartans and their allies on the other.[3]

But we must end here. To narrate how those who stood together in one generation become, in the next, enemies, is beyond the scope of this book.

Notes

Prologue

1. See further N.G.L. Hammond, *A History of Greece to 322 B.C.*, Oxford, 2nd ed., 1967, chs. 2–7.
2. Hdt. 3.31.
3. On the Persians see further M. Brosius, *The Persians*, London, 2006, pp. 6–78.

Chapter 1: From Cyrus to Darius

1. Brosius, *Persians* pp. 3–5; A.R. Burn, *Persia and the Greeks*, London, 2nd ed. with a postscript by D.M. Lewis, 1984, pp. 21–35. Medes and Persians were so close that many Greek writers use both terms interchangeably for the two peoples.
2. Hdt. 1.107–130 with Brosius, *Persians* pp. 8–9; L. Allen, *The Persian Empire*, London, 2005, pp. 26–27; J.M. Cook, *The Persian Empire*, London, 1983, pp. 25–43.
3. Hdt. 1.6–22, 26–56, 69.
4. Hdt. 1.53, 71–73, 75–88 with Burn, *Persia*, pp. 39–43.
5. Hdt. 1.86–88 with A. Keaveney, 'Persian Behaviour and Misbehaviour: some Herodotean examples', *Athenaeum* 84, 1996, pp. 23–48.
6. Hdt. 1.141.
7. Hdt. 1.141, 148, 152–153 with Burn, *Persia*, pp. 43–45.
8. Hdt. 1.154–170 with Burn, *Persia* pp. 45–47.
9. Burn, *Persia*, pp. 48–62, 81–93.
10. Burn, *Persia*, pp. 81–126. Cf. Hdt. 3.89 for the Persian view of the three kings.
11. Hdt. 4.1, 83–98, 102, 118–142 with Burn, *Persia*, pp. 127–133.
12. Hdt. 4.143–144, 5.1–2, 17–21 with Burn, *Persia*, p. 134.
13. Hdt. 5.12–17 with Burn, *Persia*, p. 135.
14. Hdt. 5.11, 23–24, 6.40–41, 104 with Burn, *Persia*, pp. 133 n.14, 135–136, 224–225.

Chapter 2: The Ionian Revolt (499–494 BC)

1. Hdt. 5.30–34 with A. Keaveney, 'The Naxian Expedition: "a forgotten cause" of the Ionian Revolt', *Classical Quarterly* 38, 1988, pp. 76–81.
2. Hdt. 5.35–38, 109, 6.7 with Burn, *Persia*, pp. 196–198; G.B. Grundy, *The Great Persian War*, London, 1901, pp. 89–91.
3. For all aspects of the Ionian revolt see the in-depth treatment of P.L. Tozzi, *La Rivolta Ionica*, Pisa, 1978.
4. Hdt. 5.49–51.
5. Hdt. 5.55, 73, 96–97 with Burn, *Persia*, pp. 187–188.
6. Hdt. 5.97, 99–103 with Burn, *Persia*, pp. 200–201.
7. Burn, *Persia*, pp. 201–206; Grundy, *War*, pp. 142–144.
8. Hdt. 5.124–126.
9. Hdt. 6.1–5.
10. Hdt. 6.6–20, 29–32 with Burn, *Persia*, pp. 209–217.
11. Hdt. 6.42–45; Diodorus Siculus 10.25 with Burn, *Persia*, pp. 221–222.
12. Hdt. 5.105.

Chapter 3: Marathon (490 BC)

1. Hdt. 6.48–49, 7.133–137.
2. Hdt. 6.94–97.
3. Hdt. 6.98–101, 119.
4. Hdt. 6.102, 107 with Burn, *Persia*, pp. 238–239; J.A. Lazenby, *The Defence of Greece 490–479 B.C.*, Warminster, 1993, pp. 48–52.
5. Hdt. 6.103–110 with Burn, *Persia*, pp. 239–247; Lazenby, *Defence*, pp. 52–59.
6. Suda: Burn, *Persia*, pp. 247–248.
7. Hdt. 6.110–115 with Burn, *Persia*, pp. 248–252; Lazenby, *Defence*, pp. 58–72.
8. Lazenby, *Defence*, pp. 53, 80.
9. Hdt. 6.115–116, 119–120 with Burn, *Persia*, pp. 252–253; Lazenby, *Defence*, pp. 72–79.
10. Mound: Burn, *Persia*, pp. 253–254. Haunting: Pausanias 1.32.3.

Chapter 4: Between the Invasions (489–481 BC)

1. Hdt. 7.1–4, 20 with Burn, *Persia*, pp. 276–278, 316–317.
2. Burn, *Persia*, pp. 313–317. See Hdt. 9.108–113.
3. Hdt. 7.5–18.
4. Hdt. 7.60–100, 146–148, 184–186; Aeschylus, *Persians* ls. 341–342

with Burn, *Persia*, pp. 322–332; Lazenby, *Defence*, pp. 90–96; C. Hignett, *Xerxes' Invasion of Greece*, Oxford, 1963, pp. 345–355.

5. Hdt. 7.61–99 with Lazenby, *Defence*, p. 92.

6. Hdt. 1.189, 7.22–25, 32–37, 115, 118–120 with Burn, *Persia*, pp. 318–321, 337–338.

7. Hdt. 6.132–136; Nepos, *Miltiades* 7–8 with Burn, *Persia*, pp. 258–267.

8. Hdt. 5.82–89, 6.49–50, 73, 87–93, 7.144; Plutarch, *Life of Themistocles*; Nepos, *Themistocles* with Burn, *Persia*, pp. 192, 274, 279–296; A.P. Keaveney, *The Life and Journey of Athenian Statesman Themistocles (524–460 BC) as a Refugee in Persia*, Lampeter, 2003.

9. Hdt. 7.132, 145, 148, 159, 8.1 with Lazenby, *Defence*, pp. 104–106.

10. Hdt. 7.148–152. On Cleomenes' defeat of the Argives see Burn, *Persia*, pp. 227–232.

11. Hdt. 7.153–167; Diodorus Siculus 10.33 with Burn, *Persia*, ch. 15.

12. Hdt. 7.168.

13. Hdt. 7.168–170.

14. See further our next chapter.

15. Hdt. 7.25–27, 37 with Burn, *Persia*, p. 321; Lazenby, *Defence*, p. 97; Hignett, *Invasion*, p. 97.

Chapter 5: Thermopylae and Artemisium (480 BC)

1. Hdt. 7.42–60, 100–126 with Burn, *Persia*, pp. 337–339; Hignett, *Invasion*, p. 105; Lazenby, *Defence*, pp. 114–115; Grundy, *War*, pp. 218–221.

2. Hdt. 7.172–174; Plutarch, *Life of Themistocles* 7 with A. Keaveney, 'The Medisers of Thessaly', *Eranos* 93, 1995, pp. 30–38; Burn, *Persia*, pp. 343–344.

3. Hdt. 7.125–177 with Hignett, *Invasion*, pp. 127–132; Lazenby, *Defence*, p. 117; Grundy, *War*, pp. 259–267; Burn, *Persia*, pp. 409–411.

4. Hdt. 7.175–177, 202–207; Diodorus Siculus 11.4 with Burn, *Persia*, pp. 361–362, 378–380; Lazenby, *Defence*, pp. 134–136; Hignett, *Invasion*, pp. 113–127.

5. Hdt. 7.175–176, 212, 217.

6. Hdt. 7.128–131, 173, 196–201 with Lazenby, *Defence*, pp. 115–116; Hignett, *Invasion*, pp. 107–111.

7. Hdt. 7.207–233; Diodorus Siculus 11.4–11 with Hignett, *Invasion*, pp. 141–148; Burn, *Persia*, pp. 406–422; Lazenby, *Defence*, pp. 137–148; Grundy, *War*, pp. 291–317. See also Hdt. 7.101–105.

8. Hdt. 7.225, 234–238, 8.24–25.

9. Hdt. 7.220, 226–232; Diodorus Siculus 11.11. On the legend of Thermopylae see P. Cartledge, *Thermopylae*, London, 2006, pp. 153–156.
10. Hdt. 7.179–183; Diodorus Siculus 11.12.2 with Lazenby, *Defence*, pp. 123–126; Burn, *Persia*, pp. 385–388; Hignett, *Invasion*, pp. 157–166; Grundy, *War*, pp. 321–325.
11. Hdt. 7.178, 188–192; Diodorus Siculus 11.12.3 with Burn, *Persia*, pp. 388–392; Hignett, *Invasion*, pp. 167–175; Lazenby, *Defence*, pp. 126–127; Grundy, *War*, pp. 324–326.
12. Hdt. 7.194–196, 8.4–5; Plutarch, *Life of Themistocles* 7; Diodorus Siculus 11.12.4–5 with Lazenby, *Defence*, pp. 128–129; Hignett, *Invasion*, pp. 177–178; Grundy, *War*, pp. 326–329.
13. Hdt. 8.6–14; Diodorus Siculus 11.12.6–13.1 with Lazenby, *Defence*, pp. 129–130, 138–140; Hignett, *Invasion*, pp. 182–188; Burn, *Persia*, pp. 394–399; Grundy, *War*, pp. 330–336.
14. Hdt. 8.10–11, 15–22; Plutarch, *Life of Themistocles* 8–9; Diodorus Siculus 12.13.1–3 with Lazenby, *Defence*, pp. 148–150; Hignett, *Invasion*, pp. 189–192; Burn, *Persia*, pp. 400–402; Grundy, *War*, pp. 337–339.

Chapter 6: Salamis (480 BC)
1.. Hdt. 8.24–30, 44, 50; Diodorus Siculus 11.14; Plutarch, *Life of Themistocles* 9 with Burn, *Persia*, pp. 424–427; Lazenby, *Defence*, pp. 151–153; Hignett, *Invasion*, pp. 193–198; Grundy, *War*, pp. 344–350.
2. Hdt. 8.20.
3. Hdt. 7.140–141 with Burn, *Persia*, pp. 345–349, 355–358; Lazenby, *Defence*, pp. 99–102; Grundy, *War*, pp. 233–238; Hignett, *Invasion*, pp. 441–448.
4. Hdt. 8.142–143.
5. Burn, *Persia*, pp. 364–377.
6. Recall of exiles: Plutarch, *Life of Themistocles* 11 with Burn, *Persia*, pp. 351–352; Hignett, *Invasion*, p. 409. Demaratus: Hdt. 7.239; Aristides: Plutarch, *Life of Aristides* 1–7.
7. Hdt. 8.40, 71–72; Plutarch, *Life of Themistocles* 9 with Burn, *Persia*, pp. 428, 432–433.
8. Hdt. 8.40–41; Plutarch, *Life of Themistocles* 10; *Life of Cimon* 5; Diodorus Siculus 11.13.3–4 with Lazenby, *Defence*, pp. 154–155; Burn, *Persia*, pp. 361, 428–432; Hignett, *Invasion*, pp. 198–200.

9. Hdt. 8.51–55 with Burn, *Persia*, pp. 433–436; Lazenby, *Defence*, p. 155.

10. Hdt. 8.23–25, 41, 66; Diodorus Siculus 11.14.5 with Burn, *Persia*, p. 427.

11. Hdt. 8.56–63; Diodorus Siculus 11.15.2–4; Plutarch, *Life of Themistocles* 11 with Lazenby, *Defence*, pp. 156–162; Burn, *Persia*, pp. 440–447; P. Green, *The Greco-Persian Wars*, California, 1996, pp. 163–165, 168–171.

12. Hdt. 65, 67–76, 93; Diodorus Siculus 11.15.2; Plutarch, *Life of Themistocles* 11, 12; Nepos, *Themistocles* 4; Aeschylus, *Persians* ls. 355–360 with Green, *Greco-Persian*, pp. 176–180; Burn, *Persia*, pp. 441–449; Lazenby, *Defence*, pp. 156–172; Hignett, *Invasion*, pp. 201–217; Grundy, *War*, pp. 355–381.

13. Hdt. 8.76, 85; Diodorus Siculus 11.19.1 with Hignett, *Invasion*, p. 231; Lazenby, *Defence*, p. 187.

14. Hdt. 8.64, 78–82; Plutarch, *Life of Themistocles* 12; *Life of Aristides* 8 with Burn, *Persia*, pp. 454–455; Lazenby, *Defence*, p. 188; Grundy, *War*, pp. 388–391; Hignett, *Invasion*, pp. 408–411.

15. Hdt. 8.83, 90.

16. Hdt. 8.84–95; Plutarch, *Life of Themistocles* 13–15; *Life of Aristides* 9; Aeschylus, *Persians* ls. 353–432, 447–471; Diodorus Siculus 11.18–19.1–3; Nepos, *Themistocles* 4 with Lazenby, *Defence*, pp. 178–197; Hignett, *Invasion*, pp. 230–239, 411–414; Burn, *Persia*, pp. 455–466; Grundy, *War*, pp. 382–405.

17. Hdt. 8.97–110; Diodorus Siculus 11.19.4–6; Plutarch, *Life of Themistocles* 16; Nepos, *Themistocles* 5 with Hignett, *Invasion*, pp. 240–243; Lazenby, *Defence*, pp. 198–203; Grundy, *War*, pp. 408–416; Green, *Greco-Persian*, pp. 201–208.

18. Hdt. 7.236, 8.26, 93, 113–120, 126–129; Diodorus Siculus 11.27.2–3; Plutarch, *Life of Themistocles* 17–18, 21 with Lazenby, *Defence*, pp. 203–204; Burn, *Persia*, pp. 488–491; Grundy, *War*, pp. 416–420; Green, *Greco-Persian*, pp. 208–214; Hignett, *Invasion*, pp. 243–244.

19. Diodorus Siculus 11.27.3; Plutarch, *Life of Themistocles* 17 with Burn, *Persia*, p. 491; Hignett, *Invasion*, pp. 275–278.

20. Hdt. 8.113–120, 126–129; Aeschylus, *Persians* ls. 480–514 with Burn, *Persia*, pp. 497–499; Lazenby, *Defence*, pp. 205–208; Green, *Greco-Persian*, pp. 217–219.

Chapter 7: Mycale and Plataea (479 BC)

1. Hdt. 8.131–132, 9.90–107, 114–121; Thucydides 1.89; Diodorus Siculus 11.34–37 with Hignett, *Invasion*, pp. 247–263; Burn, *Persia*, pp. 547–554; Grundy, *War*, pp. 522–533.

2. Hdt. 8.133–136, 140–143, 9.1–11, cf. 5.17–21, 7.173; Diodorus Siculus 11.28; Plutarch, *Life of Aristides* 10 with Lazenby, *Defence*, pp. 211–216; Grundy, *War*, pp. 436–444; Hignett, *Invasion*, pp. 278–286; Burn, *Persia*, pp. 499–507.

3. Hdt. 9.12–18; Diodorus Siculus 11.28.3–6, 29.1, 30.1 with Lazenby, *Defence*, pp. 217–220; Grundy, *War*, pp. 444–451; Burn, *Persia*, pp. 509–512.

4. Hdt. 9.12–89; Diodorus Siculus 11.29–33; Plutarch, *Life of Aristides* 11–20 with Burn, *Persia*, ch. 24; Lazenby, *Defence*, ch. 9; Hignett, *Invasion*, ch. 7; Grundy, *War*, ch. 11.

Epilogue

1. Hdt. 9.86–88.
2. Burn, *Persia*, pp. 545–546, 556–564.
3. R. Meiggs, *The Athenian Empire*, Oxford, 1972.

Bibliography

Ancient Sources

Aeschylus, *Persians*

Diodorus Siculus, *Universal History*

Herodotus, *Histories*

Cornelius Nepos, *Lives*

Pausanias, *Guide to Greece*

Plutarch, *Parallel Lives*

Thucydides, *History of the Peloponnesian War*

Secondary Literature

L. Allen, *The Persian Empire*, London, 2005

M. Brosius, *The Persians*, London, 2006

A.R. Burn, *Persia and the Greeks*, London, 2nd ed. with postscript by D.M. Lewis, 1984

P. Cartledge, *Thermopylae*, London, 2006

J.M. Cook, *The Persian Empire*, London, 1983

P. Green, *The Greco-Persian Wars*, California, 1996

G.B. Grundy, *The Great Persian War*, London, 1901

N.G.L. Hammond, *A History of Greece to 322 B.C.*, Oxford, 2nd ed., 1967

C. Hignett, *Xerxes' Invasion of Greece*, Oxford, 1963

A. Keaveney, 'The Naxian Expedition: "a forgotten cause" of the Ionian Revolt', *Classical Quarterly* 38, 1988, pp. 76–81

——, 'The Medisers of Thessaly', *Eranos* 93, 1995, pp. 30–38

——, 'Persian Behaviour and Misbehaviour: some Herodotean examples', *Athenaeum* 84, 1996, pp. 23–48

——, *The Life and Journey of Athenian Statesman Themistocles (524–460 BC) as a Refugee in Persia*, Lampeter, 2003

J.A. Lazenby, *The Defence of Greece 490–479 B.C.*, Warminster, 1993

R. Meiggs, *The Athenian Empire*, Oxford, 1972

A.J. Podlecki, *The Life of Themistocles*, Montreal, 1975

P.L. Tozzi, *La Rivolta Ionica*, Pisa, 1978

Index